Ishmael Khaldi

A SHEPHERD'S JOURNEY

The story of Israel's
first Bedouin diplomat

A Shepherd's Journey
ISBN: 978-965-555-473-1

Text and Photographic Copyright © 2010 Ishmael Khaldi

Written and Published by
Ishmael Khaldi
P. O. Box 2064
Khawalid 20299 Israel

Email: Ish20299@hotmail.com
Website: www.ishmaelkhaldi.com

Editor
Michael Lavigne

Cover Design
Richard Silverstein

Production
Prestige PrePress

Printed in the United States

To my parents

Fatmah and Mhimad Khaldi,
the wonderful couple who raised us, eleven kids,
and who made me the man who I am today!

Contents

Preface

As I sit here today, looking across the green expanse that reminds me so much of the Galilee in winter, I realize it is exactly two years since I arrived in San Francisco as Israel's Deputy Consul General to the U.S. Pacific Northwest, and a few days away from the inauguration of Barack Obama as the first African-American U.S. President. It is time, I decide, to write this book: an account of my experiences as an Israeli diplomat, and a Bedouin and a Muslim.

I am the first Bedouin diplomat in Israeli history. Some would say that is an impossibility. Some would say a miracle. For me, it is just my life.

I'm aware this book may create controversy and raise many questions and issues of a political nature, questions worth a much longer book. I am actually working on such a book, but the present volume isn't about politics and it's not about war and conflict, nor is it about economy and culture. It's about all of these things rolled into one, as seen through the story of my growing up as a shepherd in a small Bedouin village in northern Israel, and the winding path that brought me to the place where I am today.

It will seem odd to some that I am a loyal Israeli – more than loyal. I love my country. I hope this book will show not only why this is possible, but why it's so important for my own people and for the Middle East in general. I am also a loyal son of the Bedouin, and much of my life has been focused on improving the lives of my people and other minorities in Israel. I live in two worlds – more than two worlds, really – Moslem and Jewish, East and West, modern and traditional, secular and religious. All these things exist within me, and so much of my journey has been a discovery of who I am, and how I can fully embrace all these parts of me.

I escaped the destiny of a poor shepherd boy born to a Bedouin family in the tiny, remote village of Khawalid. With my parents' help, I was the first of my family to travel to America, the first to be educated in a university, to work at the American Embassy in Tel Aviv, to travel the world lecturing about Israel and finally, to join the foreign service of a country defined as a Jewish State. Yet today, at 38, I am still a shepherd at heart. The values I grew up with – the love of hospitality, the desire to wander, the wisdom to settle differences and share resources, and the firm belief in the goodness of my fellow man – are with me still. I may be multilingual, multicultural, and a bit more aware of what's really going on in the world than most of my peers from my village, but the lessons I learned as a child are the ones that got me where I am today. I think these very same values can change the world for the better.

I believe that my future children, my nieces and nephews, and all Bedouin children, will grow up just like me, proud to be Israelis, proud of their heritage, and empowered to speak up and join forces to serve and evolve our community.

And so, from the faraway land of California, above the famous Golden Gate, I reflect on the land of my childhood, and the future that lies ahead.

January 2009
The hills of Marin County, Northern California

Acknowledgments

Publishing this book could not have been possible without the support and effort put in by a few individuals. I would like to acknowledge and thank the following people:

...My close friend Tricia Gibbs for her wonderful support and encouragement.

...My friend Jeff Saperstein who initially encouraged me to write this book.

...Dick Berman who escorted me through my days in San Francisco.

...Michael Lavigne for his continuous help and his advice to write more and more, and especially for editing the entire manuscript.

...Rich Silverstein and his team for their tireless efforts on the cover design. I sincerely appreciate how they stuck by me during the long months in which I wrote and finished this memoir.

...Paul Curran for creating the portrait image on page 131 of this book.

Chapter 1
First, Being a Bedouin

I was born the third of eleven brothers and sisters, in Khawalid, a small Bedouin village nestled on the hills of the western Galilee. Khawalid was a backwater, a somewhat forgotten village situated far from its nearest neighbors, a collection of the small huts and tents that had popped up more or less spontaneously in the 1950s. Each family in the village had its own dairy and its own flock of goats, sheep or cows. In early evening it would be very silent, till midnight when the rooster would start its cock-a-doodle-do, reminding us we were all alive and happy. At dawn, it would be the animals' turn to make noise – the baa-ing of sheep and lowing of cows waiting to be milked and fed and taken to pasture in the hills and mountains round about. In those days – this was the mid-1970s – we mostly still lived in tents, as our forefathers had for thousands of years. The Bedouin tent is an extraordinary thing. Traditionally made from goat hair, it provides great shelter from the rain and wind. It keeps you remarkably warm and dry in winter and at the same time keeps cool throughout the hot summer days. Goat hair seems to absorb whatever the weather throws at you. Our tent consisted of two rooms: one reserved for men and guests and the other for the women – which also doubled as the kitchen. We kids, both boys and girls, also lived in the women's side. The "kitchen" contained no stove, only a small hole lined with three stones in which my mother would kindle the fire. At some point we also had a gasoline-powered machine called a Primus Stove –

a great modern convenience! Everything for the kitchen was stored and kept in that one room, including the food, the cooking utensils and the serving dishes.

Only years later, when I was eight, did we move from the tent to a small house we called a *barrakiya*. Bedouins borrowed the idea of the *barrakiya* from their Jewish neighbors in the kibbutzim who built little wooden houses like they used to have in Eastern Europe. They were simple to assemble, quite small, with walls made of wood and a roof of metal. Everyone in the village would gather and within a few days you'd have your *barrakiya*. Alas, the roof became very hot in the summertime, making it attractive to all kinds of little insects and scorpions ... but it was wonderful in the winter, plus we could always enjoy the patter of rain drops on the metal roofs. This movement to modernity, setting down roots in a town, was the most important change in Bedouin life in centuries, and is still going on.

To better understand my references throughout this memoir, let me begin by giving you a brief background of what a Bedouin is, what Bedouin culture is, and what our position is as Israeli citizens.

A Bedouin is a *badiya* person. *Badiya* means desert in Arabic. Originally, Bedouins were desert dwellers. Bedouins are a tribal society in which the entire tribe is composed of members from one large family. Each tribe is traditionally headed by a leader, or *mukhtar* (not unlike a tribal chief in Native American society). The *mukhtar* is appointed by consent of all the tribal members. He must be an older male, with significant life experience. In the past, the *mukhtar* was the sole spokesman and primary decision maker of his village, and liaison to government authorities – a role that was instituted during the Ottoman rule, and continued under the British Mandate and to some extent even today. He is also a mediator of disputes between families, which in modern times is his most important role, although even this is disappearing.

Bedouin society is remarkable for its strong social structure, in which the commitment of each member to his fellow tribesman is paramount, as in the *Three Musketeers*: "All for one, one for all." My cousins are an extension of myself. I can't humiliate or hurt them. To do so would be hurting myself. Mutual respect is our basic value.

Bedouins are Muslims and part of the Arab culture. But because we have always been nomads, we were unable to practice religion like villagers who are settled in one location. Moving from place to place didn't allow us the opportunity to build a mosque for daily prayer. We are often compared to Reform Jews or "secular" Muslims, because throughout the years we developed our own set of tribal and religious rules – common codes based on the social norms of each tribe. For instance, during *Ramadan*, the month when Muslims fast until evening, families in our village do cook and take coffee during the day, and indeed some, perhaps even most of us, don't fast at all.

While basic and mutual respect is the core value of our code, it is Bedouin hospitality that is by far our best-known attribute. When people speak of a "Bedouin," they speak of our hospitality. I think our famous hospitality – even an enemy is safe and well cared for if he is in your tent – arises from the fact that Bedouin tradition makes no differentiation between people – all are equal regardless of their social status.

For centuries, Bedouins have been nomad shepherds who moved with the seasons, and our itinerant lifestyle did not facilitate cross-pollination with other cultures. It was not until we allied ourselves with the emerging Jewish State that our situation began to change. The relations between Bedouins and Jews that developed in the early years before the state was declared were quite remarkable. Nof, my grandmother who passed away in 2005 at the age of 96, even spoke some Yiddish! It was her generation that made the first connections with the Jewish pioneers (*chalutzim* in Hebrew) who arrived primarily from Eastern Europe during the 1920s, 1930s, and 1940s to build the country. In fact, those were the years that defined and designed our status as a Bedouin ethnic minority in the newly-born Jewish State, Israel. My grandmother, Nof (or Jidda as we called her), intensively interacted with her new Jewish neighbors and established close ties with them. I think this was because Bedouin hospitality includes in it the unconditional respect for others – even your enemies. When the first Jewish pioneers came to establish the Jewish State, especially during and after the Holocaust, Bedouins, in their simple way, tried to contribute to their well-being. That was the beginning of these remarkable relations. But one must also remember that for years Bedouins were mistreated by the Ottomans and then the British. Both these regimes fought against various Bedouin tribes and tried to stop them from moving through their traditional territories. Additionally Bedouins have always had cultural, social and economic disputes with the landed Arab populations (a subject we'll come back to later in this book as it personally affected me). Taking all this together, the creation of a bond between Bedouins and Jews was natural and mutually beneficial.

Today, Bedouins are one of the myriads of cultural groups in Israel. We're celebrating over six decades living as an Israeli community in our diverse tribes, and we are an important part of Israel's success story. For the last fifty years, we've built villages and have pretty much embraced the building of modern Israel while preserving our common treasures, those customs and values we've grown up with for ages: our rich heritage, our deep respect for tradition, our commitment to family. As a community we are successful, but as individuals that is not always the case.

I must be honest. Being an Israeli Bedouin minority has a few complications – modern Israeli society has its particular way of life, which is, in most cases, contrary to the Bedouin set of morals: short skirts, alcohol, gender roles – my mother wears a head scarf like every Bedouin woman, my father stops to pray five times a day, my sisters would never go to a restaurant and always helped cook our meals at home, and would never wear shorts or sexy clothing. We never went to movies or out to clubs. Out time was spent time with our families, friends and relatives. But we come up against the westernized Israeli life every single day. Opportunities are not the same for Jews and non-Jews. We have to work a little harder, struggle a little more, and overcome our cultural barriers from both sides. But what seems to work is that Israel understands it is made up of innumerable cultures that coalesce into a great country. Still, Israel's potential success hasn't fully been reached, and it will not be reached until we all learn to accept, respect and tolerate the differences that make us unique Israelis. Although lots of hard work still needs to be done, Israeli Bedouins are on the path to becoming part of the mosaic that is Israel: proud of our heritage, yet proud and loyal citizens of the state of Israel.

In Israel, Bedouins live in two main communities – those in the Negev Desert, the southern part of Israel, who number around 130,000, and those in the Galilee, the north of Israel, with a smaller population of about 50,000 people. The difference between the Bedouin community in the north, from that of the Negev, lies in their relationship with the Jewish community. While the Galilee community in the north interacted with East European Jews, the Negev Desert wasn't populated by Jewish settlements until after the establishment of Israel. The influx of Jews began slowly, with immigrants from Arab countries, mostly from North Africa – Morocco, Algeria, and Tunisia. Because of that, there is a less intimate connection between Jews and Bedouins in the south.

Each Bedouin tribe has its own set of sub-customs and dialects. In the past, these tribes competed with each other, in some cases even fought one another. This was the result of economic conflicts over the usage of pasturelands, but it also revolved around ancient animosities and differing values. Struggle was common, but so was reconciliation. At the end of the day, it was always understood that there must be reconciliation between opposing sides. The well-known concept of *sulha*, the making of peace between rival tribes, was developed by Bedouins. Generally, a third party would be called in to intervene and broker a deal between rival tribes. Once a deal was set, regardless of the issue or dispute – that decision would prevail. Each side was obligated to abide by it without any violations.

In the last few decades, as Bedouins began to settle down in Israel, a clash began between the civil rules of the state with that of tribal rules. In the vast majority of cases, tribal rules would take the upper hand. Bedouins rarely hurry to call the police. They still rely on the immediate initiative of third parties to engage and solve their problems. Our saying is, "a word from the tribal leader is worth a Supreme Court decision." And it's true. "Word" usually refers to the decision of the mediators, or the respected elders of each tribe. Giving one's word is also common, and is sacred, as when a man wants to marry a woman. In many cases, a wedding might take a few months or even a year to take place, but once a young woman is "given" or promised, the "word" must be kept. To this day, we honor the supremacy of tribal rule.

Bedouin customs are conservative when it comes to social mores and family values. We take a moderate approach when it comes to religion, although within the past few decades, as varying religions erected their houses of worship within Israel, mosques were constructed as well. In this respect, Israel stands as an example for the entire western world when it comes to the expression and practice of religious freedom.

So, what makes us different from the rest of the Arab population? A legend says that the Bedouin is born from the wind. The Arabs, or *fellahin* (which means farmers) are born from the land. Indeed, in Israel and well as the rest of the Arab world, the *fellahin* are historically the landowners; we are the shepherds, the nomads, the wanderers. We have a sense of our territory, but not ownership. Wherever we found pasture and water is where we moved and settled. But even that wouldn't last long, for as the season changed, we moved on. Today, when people ask us about the land dispute that has torn apart the entire Middle East, the Bedouin perspective has much to offer. Land is not a sacred thing. I sometimes have to remind my Jewish friends that their heritage as well, holds the sanctity of man above sanctity of land.

According to our tradition, a Bedouin man cannot live without three basic needs: cigarettes, coffee, and his wife! A famous Bedouin tale speaks about a Bedouin shepherd who was tending his flock on the hills of the Galilee and ran out of cigarettes. To fight off the urge to smoke, he began to sing to himself and force his eyes to take in the lovely landscape around him, when suddenly he spied from afar two *fellahin* down the hill, fighting and arguing with each other. The shepherd was pleased to see the men approaching, and thought to himself, "I will go see what the problem is, and while speaking with them, I'll ask for a cigarette." He ran toward the two farmers, and when he met up with them, tried his best to calm them down. He could see that they were moving a stone, each toward the other's side. He couldn't quite understand its meaning, so before it got completely out of hand, he asked for his cigarette, which, to his delight, they gave to him. Then he said, "Give me another cigarette. I will solve your problem." They agreed and gave him one more cigarette. The shepherd began to whistle and sing in front of them, then asked, "Now, what is the problem?" The first farmer claimed that the stone in question should be on the other farmer's side, while the second farmer said, "No – it should be on his!" The stone marked the border between their properties, and both felt his was supposed to be the larger. The shepherd politely listened as they cursed and shouted and argued about who owned more of that piece of land. (Bedouins are very famous for their patience!) Suddenly the shepherd dropped flat to the ground and placed his ear on the soil – and then he began to laugh! The farmers stared at him as if he was mad. "What are you doing?" they demanded. Finally the shepherd stood up, and with another hearty laugh took each of the farmers by the arm and brought them close to one other. "Friends," he said, "I have listened to you both. You both claim your property is larger than your neighbor's and the border has to be moved. But in order to be an honest judge, I also had to listen to what the land had to say. That's why I put my ear to the ground. And when I listened, the land began to laugh, saying, "I don't belong to anyone. Both farmers belong to me! They will come back one day and be buried within me!" The farmers were shocked by the answer, but understood the gravity of its meaning. They immediately shook each other's hand, crying and hugging each other. And the Bedouin shepherd? He went off to smoke his cigarettes in peace!

For me, this tale explores the real meaning of land in Bedouin heritage. People will fight over it, but in the end, they must show their humanity toward one another and the fight for a piece of land can easily be turned into a common ground where tolerance, understanding, and prosperity can flourish.

Israel is a modern society. And I must be honest and tell you that being a Bedouin in a modern society can be very confusing. We are a culture in transition and, not to put too fine a point to it, turning a shepherd into hi-tech engineer is no small challenge, and it can't happen overnight. With the help of the Israeli government, our younger generation is beginning to participate more fully in contemporary life, but gradually and carefully. Our aim is to combine the best in both worlds – tradition and modernity – into something uniquely Bedouin. Israel's acceptance of diverse cultures allows us, for the most part, to preserve our customs and live our heritage. The government's involvement is not without its failures, of course. Modernization requires adherence to the rules of a modern state, which is not always easy. When my grand-mother first began to settle into one permanent location, a village later recognized by the government, she at first refused to build a modern concrete house. She wanted to keep her tent, and then a *barrakiya*, where she would maintain her traditional lifestyle of raising chickens, goats, and sheep. The authorities' approach was: "She'll become modern if we catapult her into 'modernity' by building her a villa with a swimming pool and broadband Internet." You live in a modern environment, therefore you are modern. Naturally, for an older generation so deeply rooted in their traditions and culture, this evolution would not be possible. But we, the younger generation, are on a different path – moving ourselves toward full participation in a modern western society, as well as finding a way to stay true to our Bedouin culture, our commitment to family, and our respect for tradition.

Childhood in Khawalid

Oh how I loved my childhood in the village of Khawalid! Situated on the hills northeast of Haifa in the western Galilee, it was like an Eden for a small boy. All of us children played out our same routine every day: parading

As a child (circled), with my family

home from the elementary school in the Arab village of Ras Ali, two and a half miles away, then playing in the backyards, among the shacks and tents or in the muddy, dusty paths between them. On our luckiest days (a day off from school is a lucky day to any child!), we stayed at home and drove our parents crazy like children the world over. After school hours, we'd grab lunch quickly, and go off to take care of the family's sheep and goats on the hillsides nearby. The animals were a crucial part of the family income, and we all pitched in to do whatever work we could. In fact, I began taking care of sheep when I was five years old. We sold milk and around holidays we would also sell some of our flock for sheep and goat meat. Every morning, we had to feed the chickens, and in the evenings we would make sure they were safely returned to their coop. Whatever eggs we didn't need, we sold. Even that work had its pleasures; we loved our peaceful, pastoral lives, not only as kids but also as adults. The ideal Bedouin life is tranquil and simple. We love eating the freshest of eggs, meat, and milk, not to mention the delights of Bedouin tea.

In those days, Khawalid wasn't a formally organized or recognized village. In order to be "recognized," the authorities, mainly the Interior Ministry and the Ministry of Housing, must register you as an established village, one that needs development in terms of its infrastructure, electricity, and roads. This entails the granting of permissions to build houses and schools, and offer medical care and other municipal services. Khawalid, like other early Bedouin villages was simply a collection of small huts and tents that had more or less spontaneously appeared wherever we decided to settle. There was no electricity or running water. Our only water source was from a pipe that reached us from the nearby kibbutz orchards. Our neighbors at Kibbutz K'far HaMaccabi supplied us with this essential ingredient of life – an arrangement that lasted all the way through the 1960s. They were committed to helping us provide this basic need, and we developed great and close relations with them even before the State of Israel was established. I remember that as a child, every day, sometimes twice a day, I would help my mother carry water back to our home. We would tie two plastic jerry-cans onto the family vehicle – a well-disciplined gray donkey.

As I said, Khawalid was a backwater, with no stores for shopping or parks for the kids to play in. Although ice cream was just a dream to us children, and probably to the adults, I remember *"abu Glida,"* a tall, middle-aged man with sharp eyes and strong arms from a big Arab city, who'd come twice a week during summer, riding his Vespa, to sell us homemade iced juice – something like the shaved ice and syrup Americans get at the beach or county fairs. The cookies we had, which also served as the only candy we knew, was the *zarad*, a delicious pastry filled with dates, which my mother used to make around the holidays (and sometimes just because I asked her to). I thought I could never taste anything better than those round, plump cookies. I did not discover the amazing variety of sweets available to children in big towns and cities until I visited them as a grown man. But childhood itself was sweet in Khawalid, and the difficulties of life that come with growing only became real to me as my life expanded beyond the borders of our village.

I did well in school from the very beginning. As a result, I was always the spoiled child of our family. My father often took me with him, packed into the sidecar of his Vespa, as we rode to the nearby Jewish town of Kiryat Ata whenever there was shopping to do. In the summer, to escape the overwhelming heat, my father usually allowed us a trip to the beach. On some weekends we would visit my father's friends in nearby villages and towns. These trips were just as important in bonding our family together as the village life – to go out in the world, a family has to stick together!

Our home, until I was eight years old, was a small tent with two compartments. It was a traditional Bedouin housing arrangement: the men and older boys on one side, the women and girls on the other. Our beds, which we called *farsha*, were mattresses made from lamb's wool. My mother and the rest of the women used to make them once a year, in the early summer. I remember it as a seasonal fest. Early in the summer we used to take the sheep to the creek or a nearby stream and wash them. Later that same day, or next at the latest, we would shear them, collect and roll the fleece, pile them on the strong backs of our donkeys, and bring it all back to the creek to wash a second time. Those mattresses were very warm in the winter. Each of us would have his or her own *farsha*. It's one of things I miss most about those days.

Within the tent, the women's room doubled as the kitchen. The "kitchen" contained no stoves, only a small hole lined with three stones into which my mother would kindle the fire. In this simple kitchen, my mother and sister cooked an amazing variety of dishes – truly dishes fit for a king.

Like kids everywhere, we loved sweet things. My mother would hide all kinds of sweets – mainly fruit like bananas and apples and oranges and the occasional candy my father would bring from the stores in the big cities – that she would save in order to serve our guests, as we always had many. Often, and particularly in the winter, we would steal into the room at night in search of those hidden treats, grabbing a handful which we would then secretly gobble down. My brother, Hamudi, was very talented

Visiting our village – 1997

in this, and I always competed with him as to who could do the best job and "find" (i.e., steal!) the sweets without anyone having noticed. I remember how we would cover for each other, and each time one of us went on a candy raid, the other would stand guard and let out a warning if our mother or father became suspicious of what we were doing. One evening, however, Hamudi decided to go on a candy caper alone, without letting me in on it. All of a sudden, a set of wool *farsha* fell on him and he began to scream, stopping only when our father jumped in to help him. Of course, the big joke was that by that point, we all knew that Hamudi was on a mission! In fact, I have a feeling my parents knew all along what we were up to.

The interior of a Bedouin tent is a metaphorical mirror of the familial and social structure of Bedouin society: men always lead, women always support. The tent represents to us not only shelter, but a lifestyle of closeness, and open hospitality. Tents mean no secrets, no privacy. But also, a kind of instability – always ready to move on to the next place. Tents are small. No big wide houses with many rooms! They keep life simple. A tent is where you sleep in comfort, eat wonderful, fresh food, drink hot, delicious coffee and tea, and enjoy the bounty of family and friends.

For untold generations, the Bedouins lived a dynamic and nomadic lifestyle; and as I say, the tent is the symbol of that. But sometime in the 1950s, Bedouins in Israel began to give up the nomadic life and intensively settled in permanent villages. Not surprisingly, Bedouins settled spontaneously, and not in an organized way. There was no decision that "here we shall settle, build a school, and create an infrastructure for medical care, etc." But eventually settlement meant giving up the tent and taking a first, if transitional step into modernity.

Thus, when I was a teenager, all the families in Khawalid moved from their traditional tents into the *barrakiya*, which I've described as a small, wooden shack with a metal roof. The move from tents was gradual. In fact, even when the phase of the *barrakiya* was over and people really started to officially settle and build modern concrete houses, they missed their tents so much that many families erected a tent near their house or villa – and to this day spend most of their time in it. Nevertheless, we, the entire community, understood that our way of constantly uprooting our families was detrimental to the ability of our children to participate in society, to attend school, university, make a good living, have a career, and so on. We decided we wanted permanent housing, but as the village wasn't recognized, we would not receive help, or even permission, to build concrete or stone houses. Thus the *barrakiya* was born. My father built ours with the help of the other men in the village, just as he helped in building theirs. In the winter, it was colder than the tent had been, and in the summer, it creaked as the heat of the sun expanded the metal, and as it contracted again as evening came and with it, cooler air. It was far from perfect, but we all felt it was a huge step forward.

Our small homes were filled not only with children, but also with the values and morals our culture had developed over centuries: respect for others, commitment to family, appreciation for tradition and our heritage. Bedouin hospitality and generosity were the strongest values instilled in me by my parents. I think it's hard-wired into our Bedouin DNA. It begins with the famous Bedouin tea and *sada*, our strong and bitter coffee laced with cardamom, and extends to the well-known traditional Bedouin dish called *mansaf*, a delicious mix of spiced rice and nuts, usually topped with lamb meat. Although a typical household in Khawalid included just family members, guests often filled our home. The large meals for these gatherings and the huge amounts of food that my mother prepared amazed me then as it still does now. Our guests would customarily sit on the floor, with my family continuously serving them food. "Push it to their mouth!" my dad would often say. Neither my mother nor my sisters would rest until every guest was satisfied. The tradition of Bedouin hospitality has come to mean even more to me after experiencing hospitality outside of my home country, Israel – especially in American homes, where guests often stand and help themselves to their own food at a buffet. This is an oddity to me, even now. As a "half modern" person, I've found it very strange to watch people stand and mingle during dinner, and have felt awkward communicating with strangers and random people walking around the house. Just another challenge of living in two worlds.

Of course, balancing two of the most diverse cultures in this world, Israeli and Bedouin, that seem to have absolutely nothing in common, is not an easy task! The ones most affected by these cultural differences are teenagers. The vast majority of Israeli Bedouins today remain socially conservative and modest. Parents certainly try to emphasize these qualities in their children. Nonetheless, peer pressure, which is at its peak in teen years, has impacted our youth, and it is now taken for granted that all Bedouin teens will do everything the "normal" teenager does. Yet, some of the things that typical Israeli teenagers do can appear very offensive by the Bedouin cultural morals and norms. This was already the case when I was growing up, and is more so now. It is no wonder that the most important issue discussed within Bedouin society pertains to the difficulty of raising children in Israeli society, while preserving the essence of the Bedouin tradition and values. In terms of education, for instance, there has been a strong push forward. Because of our unsettled, nomadic lifestyle, education was not traditionally a part of our lives. When you move every few months (or even more frequently) you can't really send your children to school. In fact, we had no schools at all. But in coming to understand our Jewish Israeli neighbors, we too began to see how important education is. Without it, we would never progress, and our children would forever be outsiders without any real chance at success in the modern world. So today's Bedouin parents do the impossible to send their kids to school, and by the way, regardless of whether the child is a boy or a girl. Actually, in some cases, families give priority to girls since they seem to be more focused and disciplined with regard to their education. The problem, though, is that a modern education can come into conflict with traditional values, and a crucial goal for many parents is balancing of cultures, inculcating their children into their own heritage – their history, values, customs and even their accent (which is an important aspect of identity for various tribes). In this way the younger generation can correlate their behavior at home with what they see and hear outside. I know this requires a great deal of time and sacrifice from parents, but this is exactly what my parents did for me and my brothers and sisters. From my point of view, it is a real shame that too few parents are willing to put enough effort into their children. They don't realize that a few extra hours will go a long way. Children who are never taught the basic Bedouin traditions and customs will grow up to find that there is a great barrier between themselves, their families, and their homes. They will find, at some point, that they will no longer be able to diagnose their problems and feelings, nor express them accurately. Hopefully our generation will do a better job of this.

When I reflect on my childhood, it's so obvious how far I have come. While Jewish kids went to schools near their homes or rode busses or cars each morning and evening to class (at least in my imagination), I walked several miles to school every day in the cold of the winter and heat and dust of the summer. After trudging home at the end of a rainy, wintry school day, we Bedouin kids were expected to drop off our book bags and go tend the sheep and goats, or fetch water from the nearby orchard. During the summers, when children in Haifa, Tel Aviv, and even the larger Arab cities would be attending summer camp or traveling abroad, we had to settle for searching for bird nests in the sweltering heat. When high school field trips were offered, there would be too many occasions when we couldn't participate, simply because there was no money to pay for it, even if the amount was trifling. I suppose, if this is one's view of growing up, one is entitled to look back on it and feel that it was a bit cruel. And the truth is, it's hard to feel equal or dare to compete with your colleagues if these situations define you. This is the burden of many Bedouin kids, and one I had to overcome, day in, day out.

Still, there was so much to enjoy in life! My elder brother Hamudi and I were what my grandmother, with her knowledge of Yiddish called "the *vilde chayes,*" which, simply put, means, "wild animals." We two would jump out of the window, sneak around outside and collect the rest of the kids from the village to play in the mud or to hunt birds on the surrounding hills. Often times, we returned exhausted, wet from the rain, caked with mud, expecting to be punished, yet my mother didn't punish us. She just washed our clothes. It still amazes me that she'd wash those dirty outfits, especially the pants, without any hint of annoyance. But perhaps she got a little bit of punishment in, because she'd always make us put our trousers back on, still wet from washing, and place us close to the fire so they would dry right on our bodies!

We all had to stay indoors in winter, but the *barrakiya* was often too confining and boring, so we boys would occasionally ask permission to play in the hay storage next door. This joy, however, came to an abrupt end when, one day, we played with fire while in the hay storage and burned the entire structure down. That was one of the scariest moments of my entire childhood. I escaped and stayed that night with my grandmother. As ever, my mother kept the peace – she solved the problem by providing my father with another reason for the fire.

Basically, she lied. (Though when my father reads this, he'll finally learn the truth!) And indeed, the loss of the hay and the shed was substantial. While we could buy more hay from the other villagers, it would mean an extra expense in either the trade of animals or, if a trade was not viable, we'd have to sell one of our lambs, calves, or goats to buy more hay. It was quite a burden of guilt I lived with that winter.

But my parents were tough as well as gentle, and were used to hardship. Every day that I can remember, my father would wake at 5:30 in the morning, prepare himself for a hard day of work at the kibbutz, and regardless of the weather, drive off in his little Vespa and later his old American-made Jeep, all to feed eleven mouths at home. My mother would rise with him every morning as well, to prepare a quick breakfast, usually nothing more than tea and the goat cheese she herself had made. She served all eleven children and my father every day of our lives. After father left and we were off to school, she immediately would go and milk the goats and cows. I often try to imagine the insanity she must have gone through in order to raise us in those impossible conditions – cooking our food over a fire that still was within our *barrakiya*, or baking pita bread or preparing larger meals on a fire outside. Each summer, we would collect enough firewood to heat the stoves and water for all the household uses, not to mention enough to warm our house for the entire year. The winters were cruel and harsh, always rainy and muddy. In those days, children were usually kept inside around the fire, which had to be tended, often by my mother, to ensure that it wouldn't die out. To add insult to injury, even during those harsh winters, all bathing and showering was done with cold water; firewood was too precious to waste on the luxury of warming water for a bath. (Perhaps this was the reason that, years later, I loved swimming in the freezing cold water of the San Francisco Bay!)

My childhood was hard, but also wonderful and carefree. Even so, my parents knew, as I did later, that my future did not lie within boundaries of Khawalid. Looking back today, I realize that from the beginning there were hints that my adult playgrounds would be far from the hills and mountains of the Galilee. My father would always say, "Ish, I want you to attend university and visit the White House." He didn't really know what the White House was. He just saw it frequently mentioned in the news and knew it was a powerful institution. Of course, America was a big name to us all, and later when it would become closer and reachable, we realized (in a painful but also funny way) how elusive and unreal the image portrayed on TV was. Our little 14-inch black-and-white television was the first and only one in our village. Since there was no electricity, we powered it with the Jeep battery. Every night, the entire tribe gathered in our tiny *barrakiya* to watch TV. Some programs were in Arabic, some were in Hebrew, and we also watched news and programs from America. (Later in life I would come to realize how wrong and unfair it is to judge a country only by what you see in the media. But more of that later, when we talk about how people see Israel, which is, of course, mostly through the media.) But for now, the TV and our imagination was all we knew about America. Even as a kid, I was dazzled by the idea of one day seeing this powerful, distant place for myself. I was certain I would eventually make it there because from a very early age, the course of my life seemed to be a path out of Khawalid. This began right away, with elementary school, which was in another town, Ras Ali, and this trajectory continued through high school and university. In fact, my father had this very plan in mind for me. Of all my brothers and sisters, he decided I was best suited for in school. And it was true. I was always very curious and ambitious, and my potential appeared greater than that of my siblings and my friends in the village. My father was determined to create a better future for me. Even my teacher, Omar Sumrei (God bless his memory), would say said to me, "Ya, Ish! Your place is in the Orthodox College at Haifa!" referring to the famous Christian Arab high school, considered to be the most prestigious Arab secondary school in Israel.

The road out of the village was not a straight line. There were lots of barriers, lots of curves, and lots of heartache. Take for example, my elementary school in the Arab village of Ras Ali. In those days, the village, Khawalid had not yet been recognized by the Israeli government, so we didn't have a school of our own, a Bedouin school. Thus we had to enroll in the school in Ras Ali. To an outsider, it would seem to be no problem, but Bedouins and villagers are not always the best of friends. In fact, we kids had tense relations with the local kids of Ras Ali. These were *Fellahin*, landowners. We were pastoral nomads. Legend has it that the Arab *Fellahin* are born from the land, and the Bedouin are born from the wind – and sometimes farmers don't like it when the wind blows too hard! Naturally we fought and clashed with the *fellahin* kids. Our teachers tried to teach us that we were all of the same culture and all equal to one another, but the *fellahin* looked down on us. Our accent was different; our sense of humor; our clothes – just about everything.

Fellahin were like rocks. They stuck to one place, even in their minds. We Bedouin liked to move and roam, and our attitudes reflected that. In Bedouin life, you wander around and settle wherever you find grazing area and water for the herds, and even if that movement is conscribed to an area not much larger than 10 miles, as it was with our particular family, the nomadic lifestyle formed the basis of our identity, our way of looking at and perceiving life. For instance, even though my parents "settled down" as I described, for years they still found themselves moving seasonally. Things that are permanent, structures, cities, objects, even mosques, have little value for us. On the other hand, the things that give life and sustenance are more precious than gold. A Bedouin will rarely fight for land, but will do whatever is necessary to secure water. In some odd way, we were closer to the society of the kibbutz, with its ethic of sharing and growth. In any event, we and the *fellahin* kids would have daily scraps and fights. It seemed to never end. The worst fight would always take place on the last day of each semester when we received our seasonal diplomas. Whichever group won the fight were considered the leaders of the school for the following semester. These were serious altercations and sometimes children were hurt, but we were kids being kids, and I don't believe the fights were truly motivated by any deep animosity for each other; we were just establishing a pecking order within that small, and somewhat dysfunctional, social sphere. We Bedouins place a very high value on respect and pride. We were not about to let any *fellahin* kid take that away from us.

On top of juvenile misbehavior, the school building itself was a "crime." Its metal shell caused it to be unbearably hot in the summer, forcing us to often conduct classes outside, in the shade of a tree. In the winter, it was cold and noisy. It was horrible, to be honest, and eventually I made myself the leader of a little protest movement about the conditions there: too cold, too hot, unsafe, no water, and so on. I was always being brought in to face the school administrators. Eventually, though, I became a friend of Mr. Hamid Awwad, the principal who established the school. He was an Arab educator who would frequently delegate me as class leader in the absence of teachers. But also, he would give me the job of climbing the nearby hills with a few other kids to pick wild mushrooms, mint, and zatar leaves. I earned enough of his trust that he finally gave me a mission of great importance – one that fit in very well with my protest movement. One day he called me into his office and said, "Ish, the Minister of Education, Arbeli Almozlino, is coming to the village and to our school to test the students and examine the conditions here. She will have cameras and reporters from Channel 1. I want you to collect your troops (he meant the other kids) and protest in front of the camera so they can see how bad it is here."

I was extremely excited. This was exactly the type of activity I had always wanted to do. A real protest! In front of cameras! I gathered my "soldiers" and prepared my "action." On the day of the official visit, the minister arrived with her TV team, and they began to inspect the school. Suddenly, there we were – shouting our slogans at the top of our lungs, and then, as I planned, began throwing stones at the roof above the classrooms, and pretty soon we started tossing the tables and chairs around and in general vandalizing the entire school! Mr. Awwad came running toward us, shouting in front of the camera and calling my name. I saw the look on his face. It was so serious and angry. I didn't know what to think. With the TV camera and minister looking, he came right up to

me and angrily demanded to know what we were doing and
why we were behaving in this manner. Without hesitation
I said, "You, Mr. Principal ... You told us to do this in front
of the camera!"

Poor Mr. Awwad. I guess he didn't know what he
was in for when he asked a Bedouin for help.

But our Arab teachers were truly wonderful and dedicated. Most of them drove many miles from their Arab
villages over rough roads to get to our school. Even then
I admired their sacrifice. Ras Ali was a remote village.
The crude road to it was a mess of muddy terrain, so rough
that cars could hardly navigate it, and when the teachers
arrived they had to work in a school that was really just a
shack with a metal roof with no water or electricity. These
teachers could easily have worked in their own towns, but
they drove ten, fifteen, twenty miles each way, every day.
They chose us. And I will always be eternally grateful to
each and every one of them.

In spite of our differences, I did come to realize that
we Bedouin were one with the Arab kids. This lesson
was a landmark in my search for an identity. Or, perhaps
it was a major ingredient in my having a split identity. I
always considered myself a Bedouin – a proud Bedouin, yet
was I not also Arab? And a Muslim? We don't practice
religion like the *Fellahin* – we don't build mosques, and we
don't have *mullahs* or preachers. What we have is a set
of morals, of tribal rules that serve as guiding principles
in our lives. Our Islam is different from the more settled
forms of Islam practiced by other Arabs – but in the end,
are we not all brothers?

Of course the Arab kids returned home after school
to nice houses with electric heat and electric light and lots
of things to do in their towns, while we came home each

day to find our herd of goats waiting to be taken care of. In the evenings, we all gathered around the oil lantern that provided a bit of light for us to do our homework. There was no privacy or quiet, which made it almost impossible study for exams, though I have to admit I loved the intimate feeling of huddling together in study. I also found it hard to stay awake after our long, exhausting day. No wonder my parents had a hard time convincing me, a poor Bedouin kid, that education was the most important thing for my future and that I had to invest all this time and energy on something so difficult and with a reward that seemed so very far away.

More than once on a winter's day, my friends and I would slip away to the hills surrounding the school and skip all our classes. In the afternoon, when the rest of the students were on their way home, we would join them for the trek back to the village. Our parents didn't have a clue, which was a good thing, because most of the time it was my idea to skip school. I not only agreed with the other kids from my village that there was no point in going to school – especially with *fellahin* and in such a rotten building – as I was actually a ring leader. As far as we were concerned, it was better to stay home and help our parents with the livestock and perhaps go to work at the kibbutz to help support our families.

Somehow though, in spite of all this, my curiosity and love of learning got the better of me, and I ended up a star pupil.

In 1984, I began high school in the city of Haifa. This move was the first dramatic change in my life. Earlier that year, at the suggestion of my beloved teacher, Omar Sumrei, I applied to the Arab Orthodox College in Haifa. It was a tough place to get accepted into, but I managed to pass, and was, in fact, one of the few students accepted. I was certainly pleased, but my father was *elated*. His talented son was now on the right course toward a higher education. I was also quite nervous. It frightened me to be so uprooted from my village, having to take this daily journey to a strange, new place, a big place – a city! I took solace in the fact that I would return home every evening, and could still visit the kibbutz and Kiryat Ata for haircuts, medical care, and new clothes. But for the first time in my life, I felt lonely.

At first I hated the Orthodox School. It took about three seconds to realize the huge gap between myself and the other students. I had been warned that they came from the higher class of Arab society in Israel and that I would be the only Bedouin student in school – a shepherd, the son of shepherds – but to hear of it and to experience it are two different things. The difficulty came not only from my Bedouin accent, which the other students didn't understand, but their way of thinking and looking at me. And, here again, came my question of self-identity: If we're the same, belonging to the same Arab culture, then why do they think of me as a stranger? I adjusted gradually, but never truly felt as if I belonged. In the village, you know who your friends are. In the wider world it's more complicated. During those difficult high school years, I came to understand what real friends do, how they keep in touch no matter what, how they help in troubled times, how they share both joy and grief – and how most of the people you meet won't ever be true friends. It was perhaps the hardest lesson of all: not to apply the same expectations of friendship to those who weren't brought up in the same way I was.

One of the most painful and confusing issues I had

to deal with was my place in Israeli society, which is really quite different from non-Bedouin Arabs, and one *fellahin* Arabs could not easily understand. Bedouins take pride in the fact that they have helped build the modern State of Israel: we formed strong bonds with the first Jewish pioneers, and we feel that we belong to Israeli society and are part of the nearby kibbutz life. The way my classmates viewed Israel was quite different, even though, to my mind, it is their country, too, and this was outrageous to me. Most of the kids affiliated themselves with the various Palestinian national movements, and it became especially vocal when we studied Israeli political institutions and structure. My neighbor in that class kept a Palestinian flag. He thought of himself as a Palestinian Arab living in Israel. I considered myself a Bedouin Israeli. As you can imagine, there is a great divide between the two.

I later came to understand that their views came from the education they received at home. The school itself was an Arab Christian high school, run by a private institution. It focused on humanities and pure science studies. There were no classes in religion. The teachers maintained neutrality on issues of politics. So anti-Israeli sentiment was not taught. It simply was. I found this disturbing then, and I do now – more so now, in fact, when I see the damage this has done to everyone.

Going to high school in Haifa was the beginning of the end of my childhood. It was my first real exposure to the larger political world of Israel and the world outside my village. The experience made me, after a time, a more independent person. As for the painful things I experienced in school, I told my parents nothing; I kept bottled up inside the sadness I felt about how the other students treated me.

Fourteen-year-olds are often cruel, especially when they hang out in small gangs. They like to pick a victim. To them I was perfect. I didn't speak with the same accent, didn't wear the same fashions. They were brutal creatures. They either ignored me or called me names. When I tried to tell a Bedouin joke, they decided they couldn't understand my accent and didn't laugh. And though I was a great runner, and they respected me for that, I often ran barefooted, which of course they thought primitive.

My most cruel memory was on Israel's Memorial Day, the day before Israeli Independence Day. I drew a great deal of attention to myself by standing outside the class for the minutes of silence. This outraged my fellow students. Why was I standing, they wanted to know? "The Bedouins standing with Israel are traitors," they taunted. I felt miserable, but I stood there all the same. I am, after all, a proud Bedouin. And proud that my brothers Hamudi and Amin were at that time serving in the Israeli Army.

How amazing that I felt at home in the nearby Jewish kibbutz, but in this Arab school, where we shared the same culture and language, I felt foreign and threatened. In time I learned to play their game and get along, but this period of school, especially the first two years, was like an exile to me – living life as a stranger, not belonging to the people I was supposed to belong to. This only strengthened my ties to my village and my life as a child growing up near the kibbutz.

Although I was too young to fully comprehend it, I was observing society through the prism of two worlds. From circle to circle, I was always searching for a way to belong, but could never quite find my way in. I stood in some crossroad between all these different cultures, societies, religions, and languages. That never-ending search for belonging inevitably brought me back to the same conclusion: I am a true, genuine Bedouin. I belong to nowhere, my roots are no roots, and my real people are my tribe. But I knew that I would have to "swim in strange, dark water," as we say, in order to move resolutely into the future. The way back to the village was closed to me. I had already travelled too far. My fate was to continue this journey, a shepherd's journey, into the wider world, to seek new horizons. That is where real life would begin for me.

But even though I was less connected to my village, I understood it would always live within me. The people of my village were my foundation.

My family was my pillar. During those years, I often saw my mother do the impossible to help me. When I needed money, she never hesitated to support me. Even when she had no money or not enough for all of the family's needs, she made sure I had enough. I never had less than my classmates. It's ironic, but by excluding me, my high school classmates helped me better understand my true identity as a Bedouin and, paradoxically, accept that my colleagues and teachers at the Orthodox Christian high school were also part of me, just as were the kibbutzniks of Kiryat Ata and the *fellahin* of my grammar school. It led me to confront the central question in my life: Who am I? And I answer: Bedouin, Israeli, Muslim, Arab, shepherd, scholar, and now, diplomat.

Chapter 2
America!

I t was summer of 1990 when I first decided to visit America, a few months after graduating from the Orthodox Christian College High School in Haifa. My older brothers, Amin and Hamudi, were IDF soldiers then, and I wanted to follow suit eventually. They both served as trackers in the northern command, on the Lebanese border. I also wanted to volunteer for the military, but my parents urged me to continue my studies first. "Ish," they said, "finish your studies, then do whatever you want." You have to understand that formal education was not traditionally a core part of our nomadic society, so you might conclude it was somewhat remarkable that my parents felt that way. Bedouin parents today do everything in their power to send their children to university.

I agreed to attend college, but I set a condition: I would take a year off before resuming my studies. It took some doing to persuade my parents, but I finally took a job at Kibbutz K'far HaMaccabi. The idea was to save some *gelt* for college studies. (Again, my grandmother's Yiddish is how I put it!) We were eleven brothers and sisters, and I didn't want to be a burden to my parents. My mother never earned money – she was the original stay-at-home mom, and though by this time my father worked at a chemical firm near Haifa, he earned only a modest income.

Our village had an excellent relationship with the kibbutzniks and my late grandmother, Nof, was considered practically family to the kibbutz pioneers whose names

My Grandmother   *My Father*   *My Mother*

have come down to me: Shraga, Tuvia, and Zeev Raban. She worked with them when they first began cultivating the fields in the area and when they planted the citrus orchards that now surround the kibbutz. Many Bedouins from the area worked for the kibbutzim as agricultural workers.

I started work in Solit, a rubber factory at K'far HaMaccabi, as a press machine operator. My shift started at 4:30 a.m. and I worked until 12:30 p.m. I was full of motivation and excitement. This was my first chance at independence. At that time, Khawalid still had no electricity. Each day, I would awake by 4:00 a.m., wash and dress in the dark, and walk in the early morning before sunrise through the mud of the winter to my job. But I enjoyed working at the kibbutz. It was the dream of every young man in Khawalid to have a job close to family, plus I worked alongside six of my cousins – it was almost like I never left home!

Four months after I began at K'far HaMaccabi, I had the good luck to meet several young Jewish students who had come from Canada and a place called White Plains, New York to volunteer at the kibbutz in order to learn Hebrew and immerse themselves in Israeli society, culture, and politics. They were all my age, in other words, between high school and college. We made an immediate, heartfelt connection. It was with them that I started speaking English. It was the first time in my life I met people from America or any country that was not Israel. Remarkably, these total strangers turned out to be just like me and my friends: polite, curious, and energetic. I invited them to Khawalid and my parents welcomed them into our home – in fact, were proud of the friendships their son was making. Very soon, our connection grew closer and more intimate – something far beyond what you might expect from co-workers at the kibbutz. Soon I was inviting them to weddings and engagement parties in the village so they could learn about our culture and heritage. They also invited me to their dorms in the kibbutz, especially the Friday nights during the summer, where we'd sit outside to listen to music and dance in the little pub dedicated to the overseas volunteers. They also invited me to visit them at their homes in America and Canada. I loved my new companions, but I became closest to Robin, a pretty, blond, Jewish student from Canada, who taught me English from time to time. Alas, by May of that year, my friends had completed their exchange program and were about to leave the kibbutz. Before they left, they extended an open invitation to come and visit them in New York and Canada. Of course, such a dream seemed almost impossible – and yet, an invitation is an invitation – and I could not get it out of my mind.

I think I surprised even myself that I was seriously considering a trip to that distant continent, America, so far away. It was to New York that my mind wandered. I might as well have been contemplating going to the moon. Yes, me, the Bedouin boy from Khawalid, now thinking about going to New York, America, the land of milk and honey and a golden life where everyone lived in mansions – Was I crazy? America was a separate universe, and New York? – the center of the universe.

Before I knew it, I found myself driving to Haifa in a Volkswagon Beetle that my brother Amin had borrowed for me – a wild idea in itself, since gas prices were soaring in the country – but even wilder was the fact that I was going to Haifa to visit a travel agency and apply for a visa. Two weeks later, Erik from the agency called me to let me know that my visa was approved. I freaked out! The all-powerful America was accepting me and welcoming me to visit. With Erik's assistance, I bought a ticket for a flight, but kept the whole thing secret, especially from my family. I feared that if I told my parents, they'd simply say no. And besides, what right-minded Bedouin parent would believe their son would leave the family to go to America? You *never* leave the family. It's not done. I decided the best course of action was to tell them nothing until the day before the flight. Meanwhile, my friends from the kibbutz, some of whom had spent time in America or had relatives there, encouraged me to go. For them it was no big deal. They'd tell me, "There are many young Israelis in New York who left after their military service and work in moving companies," and "No need to speak good English – you'll find Israelis everywhere!" I imagined myself in a kibbutz in the heart of America. How hard could it be? The urge to travel burned like a fire in my gut. But, in reality I had no idea of how America would really look. I was taking an extreme step, beyond adventurous. To abandon my family and my country for the first time, not just to go to nearby Turkey, Greece, or Italy, but all the way across the ocean, far from everything familiar … it was unheard of for someone from my village. But

I couldn't stop myself. America! New York! I would go no matter what!

Yaniv, one of my kibbutznik friends, told me that his brother Doron and a few others from the kibbutzim in our area were living in New York. He'd talk to him and get him to help me when I arrived. I forwarded Yaniv my flight details, and he gave me Doron's telephone number. I recall how impressed I was by the long, ten-digit phone number. My new friends from White Plains and Canada had left about a month before to return to North America, but, quite honestly, I was very shy to call them. Not to mention that my purpose was to go to New York City, and I thought White Plains was hundreds of miles away. It all seemed so vast to me. (Canada of course, was a whole other country.)

Doron's phone number seemed like a good start. I knew what he looked like, and I was a friend of his brother. In Israel, friends always help one another. Mutual responsibility is a major value in Israel. The traditional Jewish saying, "*kol Yisrael arevim ze le zeh*," means all Israelis are responsible for each other.

As the date of my flight to New York fast approached, I found myself roaming the familiar hills and mountains around the village where I grew up. I knew (and still know) every stone, tree, and cave. These were the very places where, as a child, I grazed the family goats and sheep. And now I felt a deep longing, and a fear. I was going to America, the Golden Land. Who knows? Maybe I would get a green card, find a job there and all would be OK? Maybe I would attend school there and my adult life would be so much easier than my childhood in Khawalid. If so, maybe I would never come back, never live in the village again. A kind of fever came over me, and I began visiting relatives like never before. They began to worry about me – What was happening to this boy, "behaving like he'd never see us again?"

Two weeks before my flight, I approached my manager in the kibbutz, Eyal, and informed him that I would be flying to America for a month or so and needed to schedule a vacation. He approved the vacation, but immediately told the rest of the employees about my trip, including my cousins who also worked there, because he needed a temporary replacement. In a Bedouin village, news travels fast – gossip is a big part of daily life. You can't hide anything, and this particular news item immediately stirred a big noise throughout the area. Overnight, everybody had heard that Ishmael was going to America.

Now I realized what a big mistake it was not telling my parents, for in just a few days the rumor was everywhere. A friend's mother told my eldest brother Amin, who came to ask me if it was true. Instinctively, I replied, "No! It's just a rumor." He tried again the next day, but my answer was still, "No." But you can't really lie to your brother Amin – he sensed the truth and told my mother. It was day and a half before I was to leave. The next morning, right after feeding our small herd of sheep and goats, and as I was preparing to go to work at the kibbutz, my last shift before my trip, my mother approached me.

She didn't look happy. "Ish," she demanded, "Are you going to America? Everybody in the village says so, and you didn't even tell us. Tell me!"

I couldn't hide it any longer. I knew she could tell just looking at my face.

"Yes," I admitted. "I am flying out tomorrow night and will be gone for one month." I gave her all the details for my flights. (Tel Aviv to New York, midnight flight with

Tower Air, an Israeli airline, now defunct, known for its strict adherence to the kosher dietary needs of its passengers, the airline of choice for the Jewish ultra-Orthodox Hassidic community.)

To my surprise she wasn't angry. She merely told me she had always believed in me, and was confident that "whatever Ish does, he does well." I understood then, that one could not be blessed with a better, more understanding mother.

Now, however, came the problem of my father. Now that my mother knew the truth, she felt it was her responsibility to tell him. I explained to her that I was going to visit my friends in White Plains, New York, and more importantly, that I was going to check into the possibility of studying in America. I never told her that my only connection in New York City was a phone number for Doron and that I had no idea where White Plains was. If they had known that this was not a well-planned trip in search of colleges and universities, but rather an adventure to see and discover America, I am sure they wouldn't have given me permission to go, and I would have never left without their permission and blessing. I guess I played the education card because it's a top priority in the Bedouin community. Every Bedouin parent wants to provide their children with a formal, modern education. My father often told us, "I'll do anything I can to have you attend university, even if I need to sell my clothes." As for me, I swore I would never disappoint them. Now, of course, I might have been doing just that.

On the day before the flight, I finished work early to get home and complete my preparations for departure. As I walked through my village, I could see the admiration, excitement, and perhaps envy in the eyes of so many of my friends and relatives, especially the children who were staring up at me and whispering, "He's going to America," and then shouting, "Ish, take me with you!" "Ish put me in your suitcase!" Deep inside, I thought, yes, one day they too will make it; they too will have the opportunity to see the world outside our village.

At home, I found my parents, sisters, and my two little brothers already sitting, waiting for me to join them for dinner. They were all smiling and very happy, eager to hear about America and what I would find there. The entire night, my father didn't stop giving me suggestions and directions about whom I should speak to, what to – and more importantly – what *not* to do there, and so on. Well, he's a father, and even today, when I'm thirty-eight years old, he keeps pushing me: "Ish, do this, don't do that." And most of all, "Ish, get married!"

That night, I couldn't sleep. It was all too exciting, all too mysterious. Early in the morning, I drove my dad to work and took his car to do a few more errands. I was busy the entire day although not very focused. In a few hours, I would be in the air on my way to America. Me, Ishmael Khaldi, son of Fatmah and Mhimad Khaldi, shepherd, son of shepherds, on my way to the center of the world!

I said farewell to my brothers and sisters (except for Hamudi, my closest brother, who was then serving in the IDF and on duty in southern Lebanon). My mother, father, Amin and his father-in-law, a border police officer, escorted me to the airport. Tears welled up in my mother's eyes. Seeing her this way made me think of my childhood, when I would wake up early in the morning and watch her at her work. She would always say, "This is why we raise kids – to see them one day return the help and make our lives easier!" I knew this adventure of mine would be very hard on her, and though she never said a word, I knew she was despairing, "Who knows when we'll see him next? What will happen to him? What if he's hurt or feels pain far away from home? Who will take care of him?" In the meantime, my father continued to advise me what to do and where to go even though he had never been to America.

As we approached the airport, my apprehensions grew. I had only the one telephone number – I remember it to this day – (718) 646-7402, Doron's number in Brooklyn. I spoke very little English. I knew absolutely nothing about New York, or any place really, outside of Israel. Upon arriving at the airport, it took only about twenty minutes, including the security check, to be on the way to the departure gate. Tearfully, I hugged my parents, my brother, Amin, and his father-in-law. "Good luck and God be with you," I heard my parents say. And then I was gone, like the baby eagle, as we say, "proud and free." Suddenly I laughed. It was all so extreme, so huge, so different!

The flight to America was the first time I had ever been on an airplane. As such, I sat in my window seat, overlooking the airplane's wing, watching every movement of every person on the tarmac and in the plane. This experience was like visiting a new world unto itself. The plane was full of Hassidim, so easily identifiable with their long black coats, black hats, and curly sidecurls dangling from their temples. I can still remember the captain's announcements in both Hebrew and English. It all seemed so unreal. A dream. And then the realization that this was one dream that really was about to be fulfilled – flying in the air exactly as the birds I used to hunt as a child! As we approached the runway, I was conscious of the adrenaline pumping through my body. Within a minute, the giant Boeing 747, carrying three hundred and eighty tons, launched into the air. Giddy from the unsettled feeling of being in the air, as the plane banked and soared to reach its cruising altitude, I watched the twinkling city lights of Tel Aviv grow smaller, saw the expanse of the land beneath me grow larger, and the plane headed west over the sea.

It was a long flight with a stopover in Brussels and I slept fitfully. I remember how endless the flight seemed, and the flight attendant, Dafna, waking me for my meals. We had struck up a conversation and she told me that her boyfriend was from Kibbutz Ramat Yohanan, next door to my village. The world was large, but still so small. As we began our approach into New York, I watched people preparing for the end of the flight, ready to greet whatever episode was next in their life. I began hearing people around me talking about where they were heading, what their schedule was for that day after landing. I don't know how to explain the feeling that came over me then. Outside was nothing but darkness. Everyone around me had a plan. And me? I had no idea about anything. A poor boy from a small Bedouin tribe in the Galilee, who had never been to a major city in his life, was about to land in one of the largest cities in the world, probably the craziest, with no relatives, no one expecting him, only the phone number of a friend's brother and just enough money to get by in his pocket. I remembered my friends in the kibbutz asking me, "Ish, are you going to America for breakfast only? Do you think that you'll survive with that?"

The plane began its descent. The captain announced we were about to land at JFK International Airport, described the weather in New York City, and asked us to fasten our seatbelts. My heart began to pound. We banked sharply to the right and I could see highways and cars moving along them. My seat neighbor, a young Yeshiva student named Avrech, explained, "This is Queens, this is Brooklyn," names I had known from travel guides I'd read in the month before. I clutched the immigration and customs forms the flight crew had given me to fill out, having no idea what to do with them.

After landing, I watched the other passengers to learn how one disembarks. It seemed so orderly. I thanked Dafna, the stewardess, with a wish to see her again soon. Taking my cue from the others, I walked quickly toward the immigration officers, staying close to one of my other neighbors on the plane, Professor Yehoshua Feldman. Stepping up to the immigration officer, I could only hand him my empty forms. I had no idea what he was saying to me. I knew he was asking me questions, but what did he want? A Hassid in line came to help and translate. I had no destination address; the Hassid told me to write his address. I filled out the form as he instructed, handed it to the officer, and heard the thud as he stamped my passport. I was in! America embraces me, I thought. My heart raced. I was excited and frightened at the same time. I'm actually here, I thought! My first day in the land of gold and milk and honey!

At the exit door, crowds of people stood to welcome their friends and families as they streamed through the arrivals door. Flowers, hugs, and kisses were exchanged. Loving couples, who apparently hadn't seen each other for a long time, embraced amid tears and sobs. But for me, who was there? I looked around for Doron. I was certain his brother gave him my flight information and would be waiting for me. As I made my way through the crowd, my eyes searched high and low … but no Doron. He must not like crowds, I thought. So, filled with renewed confidence, I continued looking for him in other parts of the terminal.

It was still early in the morning, maybe 6:30 a.m. or even a bit earlier. After an unhappy walk around the terminal, it was clear that Doron was not there. Fine, I thought. I'll call him. After all, I have his phone number! But how to use the phone? I fumbled around until some-one took pity on me and taught me how to put a quarter in the pay phone. Now all would be well. I dialed all the ten digits of the phone number I had memorized. No answer. Perhaps no one was home? Perhaps he was here at the terminal looking for me and we kept missing each other? On the other hand, what if he had forgotten to come get me? That was my worst fear. A few minutes later, I tried again. This time, a young woman answered. I could tell from the gruffness of her voice that I had awakened her. I felt guilty, but I was desperate.

I said in Hebrew, "Can I speak to Doron, please?"

Half asleep, she answered, "Doron isn't here any-more."

"Where is he now?"

"I don't know," she replied angrily, and slammed the phone down.

I took a deep breath. This was definitely not good. Here I was, all alone, with nobody to help me in this en-tirely new world. What was I to do? Where would I go? Should I take the first plane back home to Israel? Should I pluck up my courage and keep asking for help? Keep looking for Doron? The stress and fright of the moment was tremendous, the reality of my situation hit me with full force, while all around, the noise of thousands of people milling about the terminal made everything seem surreal and threatening.

Now was the time when my tough childhood education helped me. I knew I had to stop wallowing in fear
and indecision and push on.

It was June 9, 1990, my first morning in America. I
hadn't seen sun or daylight yet and felt the need to get
out of the terminal and check the weather – to get outside the building. I rushed through the doors – only to
be met by clouds and rain and graffiti, and by the scream
of cars and jet engines. It was all shocking and depress-
ing. None of this was familiar to me. I yearned for those
sultry childhood days searching for bird nests and picking
pomegranates from the orchards around the village.

I retreated back inside the terminal. Several taxi
drivers ran up to me offering a cab. But where would I go?
Unexpectedly, I began to cry. All at once, my exhaustion
and anxiety broke open. I felt like the world was collapsing
around me, and I cried like an orphan newborn lamb whose
mother had just died. What was I going to do now? I wept
silently, searching the crowds of people, hoping to find
something or someone with whom I could communicate.
But ten minutes passed, then thirty, and still nothing. So
many people, so many languages, so many faces from all
over the world, and not one person to help me.

After almost an hour, I looked up and saw the most
familiar scene: on the second floor of the terminal, a Hassid was walking around reading a newspaper! My heart
swelled and my mood brightened immediately. I felt as if
I had been lost at sea and suddenly spotted a beacon of
light. I thought quickly: I know those people from Israel;
we have great relations with them. This Hassid is the
Messiah himself and he'll help me.

I literally ran up the escalator to reach him before

he, too, disappeared.

At first, he didn't understand what a young, tawny-skinned boy wanted from him. I tried to speak Hebrew, but he spoke only English and Yiddish. (I noticed the newspaper in his hand was in Yiddish, too.) With my broken English I finally managed to explain that I had just arrived from Israel, I was alone, stranded, and had no place to go and no one to be with. With a gentle, calming voice he said, "Don't worry. Go to Borough Park, 13th Avenue in Brooklyn. Lots of Jewish people, Hebrew speakers and Israelis. They'll help you!" He made sure that I understood him and even escorted me to a shuttle bus that takes passengers to the subway. I kept repeating the names to myself: "Borough Park, Brooklyn, 13th Avenue." I remember getting on the shuttle, sitting on the back seat, buoyed by the feeling that my real journey in America was now beginning. And, in fact, this really was the beginning of my life-long friendship with the Hassidic world, particularly Chabad.

It was now about 8:30 in the morning. From the windows of the shuttle bus, I watched the city roll past, the cars and highways, the buildings with all their graffiti. My mind couldn't unravel it all – where was the gold? Where was the milk and honey? America seemed to be exactly like Afula, Tiberias or Nahariya, towns in northern Israel. My thoughts flashed to my family back home. What are they doing now? What were they thinking? How was my mother feeling after her first day without me?

Finally, the driver stopped and looked back at me in the rear-view mirror, asking with a heavy voice, "Hey young man, this is my last stop. Where are you going?" I looked around and understood that he was talking to me since I was the only one left on the bus. He pointed to where we were on small city map, indicating this, his last stop, and quickly divined my confusion. "Go talk to those policemen and they'll explain better," he said. I got off the bus and crossed a busy boulevard, dodging the crazy morning traffic, walking toward two blue uniforms from the NYPD. Crying and confused, I asked them how to get to Brooklyn (not knowing that was where I already was). I asked for directions to 13th Avenue or Borough Park.

The policemen tried to calm me down and led me to the closest subway station. I thanked them politely and went on my own. For a moment I didn't know what to do. Standing there at the entrance to that subway station, I panicked. I knew I had to descend beneath the street. But I'd grown up in nature and knew that only foxes and rats go underground. Still, I had no other choice. Rising from the station was a terrible jumble of heat, noise, and the stench of burning metal. "Don't give up, Ish," I urged myself. "Keep going." My parents had always taught us to not give up, particularly in the toughest times. "That is your best test, Ish."

Remembering these words, I drew in a breath as if I were about to dive into the depths of some cold, dark well. Hundreds of people were pouring in and out of the station, going to work, to school, to who knows where. I descended the stairs, stopped at the gate, and then – what do I do now? The cashier noticed I was out of my element and came over, trying to explain. I couldn't understand even one word of her English, but she "understood" me, and let me enter without buying a token.

I found myself in a huge subway station where four trains came and went at the same time: two inbound (Brooklyn to Manhattan) and two outbound (Manhattan to Brooklyn). At least I knew my destination: 13th

Avenue, Borough Park, Brooklyn, and I figured that even with my poor English I could ask people to direct me to the right train. "Borough Park, Brooklyn," I said. This time, none of the hundreds of people stopped to answer. Each seemed absorbed in his or her own world, rushing to some mysterious destination. This would never happen in Israel. Israelis always stop and help, no matter who you are, no matter where you are from. (Even when Israeli's don't know the answer, they'll always say *something*, which amazingly is sometimes good enough!) But here in Brooklyn, no one would stop to help a poor boy like me. I didn't blame them entirely. They didn't know who I was or where I was from.

I tried to be patient, and became accustomed to the activity of the subway, absorbing more of the "being in America" experience. Many months later would I realize that being in New York and America are not synonymous – New York is a totally unique experience.

I watched the trains coming and going for about thirty minutes, until finally I realized that I was on the wrong side of the station, an easily corrected situation, I thought. And then one of the many miracles of my trip happened. We Israeli Bedouins look for the easiest way to do things, so instinctively, instead of walking up the stairs and crossing over to the other side of the tracks like the rest of the people, I waited for the train to leave the station, and jumped down onto the tracks searching for a quickest way to the other side. Striding back and forth along the track, I looked for a hole in the barrier that separated the two directions. Eventually I found it, raced across the many tracks and vaulted up onto the opposite platform. You would have thought that there would be screaming and yelling when people saw this crazy young guy jump down onto the tracks. But no one said a thing. Nothing. People just looked at me, some in disbelief, some with no expression at all. Not even an "excuse me, but you're going to kill yourself."

It was only a month later, when I told a new Israeli friend about my experience on my first subway ride in America, did I learn of my incredible luck to still be alive. "Didn't you think about what would have happened if you had touched one of the 'third rails' as you picked your way across the tracks?" they asked. "What's a third rail?" I said. "And how about if another train had come?" Suddenly I shuddered, envisioning a speeding train racing toward me out of the long, dark tunnel. But as harrowing as this experience was, it taught me a valuable lesson; that combining the two different worlds, living in them both, isn't an impossible mission, even if it has its problems. Both worlds can meet. I myself was making the journey between traditional heritage and the modern world, even if I was doing it all wrong and almost got myself killed. It seems to me, Khawalid and New York aren't much different from each other when it comes to human beings. It's just the lifestyle and yes, the number of people. And what I realized was, I adored this. I adored New York! And to this day, I love its life and its people and what it represents. That risky crossing – in a subway station in Brooklyn – was the beginning of my love story with America and its values, fraught with all its dangers and beauties.

But back to that first morning in America! Finally situated on the right train, I asked the conductor for help. He was a kind, older man who was very glad to help me. He quickly realized from my confusion that I was a stranger to both the city and the country. He asked me where I was from and where I was going. What currency do we use in Israel? he asked, and how much does it cost to travel by train? He seemed so nice, though I hardly understood his questions through his accent. He punctuated each question with, "See what I'm saying?" Imagine the difficulty this presented as I attempted to translate literally every word he said to me. How can you see what someone is saying? Arriving at my stop, the conductor called to me and waved me off. I climbed the long stairs up, and then – a miracle! Everywhere I looked, on signs and storefronts, and in conversation around me, nothing but Hebrew and Yiddish. I filled my lungs with fresh air, and breathed in something similar to the comfort of home. All the anxiety of the morning slipped away, and I smiled. I had arrived in Borough Park, Brooklyn.

My triumph, alas, was short lived. Because even though it looked familiar, it really wasn't. I was alone, scared, and, frankly, lost. Once again I couldn't help myself: I started crying like a lost child. I wandered into a photo store, the only place of business open at that hour. I explained in Hebrew to the owner who I was and that I had just arrived from Israel. He tried to calm me down, gave me a glass of water, and told me he wished he had come to America at my age. "Don't worry I will help you," he assured me. He had emigrated from Israel to America years before and had settled in Brooklyn. I couldn't understand why such wonderful people would want to migrate to a strange place, so far away from their own homeland. What is it about America that attracts so many people? So far, the only thing I had seen of America were dirty subways, loud highways, and lots of graffiti. The Israeli-American photo storeowner told me of a little pizza shop nearby where many Israelis meet and where I could ask someone for a place to stay. But to make sure he helped me, he called around himself and found me a family who rented small rooms. I went to the address he gave me and rented the room for $12 a night from a religious Jewish woman, living in the heart of a Hassidic neighborhood. She asked me in Hebrew about my accent, as she didn't know I wasn't Jewish. Another adventure ... a Bedouin boy from the Galilee living with a Hassidic grandmother, and feeling right at home!

I slept from noon until six or seven that evening. When I woke up I didn't know where I was or what I was doing there. After few minutes, my heart settled down and it all came back to me. I went outside the building, a three story house on the corner of 13th Avenue and 42nd Street, seeing only Hassidim running back and forth. It made me happy to see them. I felt I was among friends.

Walking around the block, I went into a clothing store and started a conversation with the owner, who turned out to be Lebanese. He said he needed some help around the store for a few days. I didn't expect any payment, but I wanted something to do – I wanted to feel I had a place to go to – and here it was. I had just arrived in the U.S., and already I had a place to stay and something to keep me busy! About a week later, I met Aviv, an Israeli distributor of milk products. He insisted on calling me Sami for some reason, which I accepted. I told him about my strange arrival a week before and he promised to help. We spent about three days together before he finally asked me where I was from. We were driving, when he stopped the car suddenly and said, "Aren't you Jewish?" When I told him no, he was extremely surprised. Everyone I had been talking with, staying with, hanging out with, had assumed I was Jewish. Though shocked, he was very respectful. I reminded him of the Bedouin with whom he had served during his years in the IDF military service. In other words, it was just normal.

After ten days in America, having still ventured no further than Brooklyn, I decided it was time to search for Doron. I called his number again, and this time a young man answered, telling me that Doron had moved, but was working at a moving company called Oddy's. When I called the company, they confirmed that Doron was indeed working there and added that they needed more people since it was summer and their busiest season. I knew I couldn't work, but the company's dispatcher, Rami, invited me to come over anyway, and he explained how to get to their office in Jamaica, Queens. With no direct train from Borough Park, I had to take a train to Manhattan and transfer to another train to Queens – a two-hour trip. As my train crossed the Manhattan Bridge, and I absorbed the wonder of the Manhattan skyline, I saw for the first time the Statue of Liberty, so beautiful and powerful, the iconic symbol and worldwide representative of America. It was wonderful. Upon my arrival to Jamaica, I walked directly to Oddy's. No sooner did I step into Rami's office, than who should appear but my friend, Doron! Naturally I was happy to see him, but by this time it wasn't that important to me. I had already been in America for two weeks and miraculously accomplished by myself all that I had relied upon Doron to help me with. He told me that he was just on his way to Chicago and would be back in a week and we could talk then.

From that moment on, I started to hang around with the guys at Oddy's, going out on the trucks with them, or staying behind with Rami. If I wanted to ride, I had to be there at 5:30 in the morning!

To get from Borough Park to Jamaica by 5:30 a.m. I

would have to leave my apartment by 3:30 a.m. I never had to do anything like this in Israel – but perhaps this was the American way! I woke up early one morning and was ready by 3:15. Outside it was dark and drizzly. As I made my way down the street to the subway station, my heart pounded with thoughts about the dangers of New York I had heard about. Just then I spied a figure walking my way, coming out from the shadows. I didn't know what to do, and I told myself, remain calm! Be nonchalant! As the distance between us lessened, I crossed the street to the other side to avoid him. At exactly the same time, he also crossed the street, and here we were, again on the same side of the street! But I could tell from his demeanor – he was also trying to avoid me! When I looked up at his face, I realized he was only a Hassid on his way to the "dawn" prayer. He had been as afraid of me as I had been of him.

A week later, a similar thing happened. At 3:20 a.m., as I climbed the stairs to the subway station, I ran into a huge man covered with tattoos. He held a small bag in his hand. Briefly, I panicked and thought, "This is it; this is the end. He will kill me here, and no one will see. No one will know. What should I do?" Once again, calling upon my childhood instincts, I decided to feign an absence of fear, and sat down near him, and struck up a conversation. I thought this might calm him down (and myself as well). As I went to sit down, my heart beating loudly in my chest, I noticed he was trying to put some distance between us. He was just as fearful of me, with my youth, dark skin, and short hair. I asked him how to get to Jamaica, Queens, knowing full well the route. When he realized I was just asking for help, he relaxed and explained which train to take and where to transfer. When the subway arrived, he led me to the train and described the route using the train map. I had crossed yet another barrier of fear.

My time at Oddy's meant going to new places and meeting new faces. I started to get more of a feel for America. I decided I wanted to move to Jamaica, Queens to be closer to Oddy's. One day, after a burglary at the offices of the moving company, they mentioned that they needed someone to stay on the lot at night and guard the trucks and vans, as well as the storage and the small office. Without thinking, I volunteered! The guys couldn't believe my craziness. They warned me that here in America, in Jamaica, Queens, I wasn't big enough or tough enough to be a guard. (Not to mention I was a volunteer!) But I was adamant. That night, I slept in the back of one of the moving vans. It was really cold and from time to time you could hear the pop of gunfire or the scream of some woman. I stayed in that truck, just praying I would survive the night.

I decided things were probably better back in Borough Park, but I really did want to stay in Queens. I found a room with a young, very religious, Yemenite Jew from Jerusalem and his American wife and their two children. This turned out to be one of my more wonderful experiences. I shared *Shabbat* dinners with them, and usually I listened to the weekly Torah portion, *parashat hashavua*. When I told them that I was not Jewish, in fact, I was a Bedouin, they were both pretty surprised – but it didn't change their feelings toward me. They did everything they could to help me, and make me feel at home. I did my share, too. I recall one *Shabbat* hearing his wife pacing back and forth between the living room and the kitchen, saying, "We have on two gas burners but we only need one." She said this over and over. At first I didn't understand what she was talking about, but by the third or fourth repetition, I realized she was speaking to me. I went into the kitchen to turn off one of the burners. As an Orthodox Jew, she was prohibited from turning off the gas on *Shabbat*, but also prohibited from asking anyone else to do it. But talking aloud to herself about the problem? What could be the harm in that! Of course she was delighted when I showed my understanding. As it turned out, having a "Shabbas goy" around – a non-Jew who could do things they couldn't on *Shabbat* – turned out to be quite an asset.

I also became friends with two Israelis living in Queens, Amir and Gadi. They were older than I and had a great deal of experience living in America. Unlike my landlords, they were secular. After a few weeks, I asked them if they needed a roommate in their basement apartment, and they agreed. As we got to know each other, they became my devoted friends and urged me to widen my horizons – which meant actually go into Manhattan and tour the city.

So one weekend, on *Shabbat*, Amir took me to Manhattan. It was quite a New York experience. In Central Park, a young kid sprang out of nowhere and demanded we give him our money. At first I thought he was just a beggar, but Amir froze in his boots – the guy had a knife pointed right at him. "Ish," Amir whispered, "we're in trouble. He'll hurt us both!" Without thinking, I jumped on our assailant, screaming at him in Hebrew and Arabic. I don't know if it was my flailing arms or my indecipherable babble, but the would-be mugger got totally flustered and ran away, disappearing back into the bushes from which he came. Amir hugged me and said, "Ish, you saved our lives. He would have stabbed us for one lousy dollar." But I couldn't have let that happen. To an Israeli, a friend is a friend, and you can't abandon your friends no matter how dangerous the situation. Responsibility for one another is at the core of our culture.

In fact, it was these very Israeli friends who pointed out to me how close to death I had been on my first day in America. One day we were waiting for a train to arrive at a subway station and we realized we were headed uptown when we wanted to go downtown. Since it was rush hour, and the place was really crowded, I said to Amir, "Let's jump to the other side of the tracks to save time." Amir looked at me as if I were a lunatic, "Jump? Jump where? Are you crazy?" It was then he told me about the third rail and about how fast the trains come out of the tunnels. I could tell he was really worried about my naiveté. But also that he cared about me.

I had now been in New York City for almost three months, and though I felt practically American, I knew it was time to return to my family. I missed my parents, brothers and sisters, tribe, and friends. I missed home. I missed Israel. I ached for my village of Khawalid and the hills around it. Strange as it may sound, despite being immersed in one of the greatest cities in the world, I missed our goats and the hours and hours I spent chasing them around the hills. I sighed with longing when I thought about sharing coffee with my friends or how I missed a number of weddings that took place during my absence. I found myself trying to remember just what it was that had drawn me to such a lonely and dangerous place so far from home. Did I find that or drink that milk and honey? Yes, in some ways I did, but the tug in my heart could not be resisted – home – where it was quiet; peaceful; safe.

I could tell my father continued to worry about me. When I made the occasional call from America to my father at work (as I said, there were no phones in the village) he never failed to urge me to take care of myself and be wary of the people that I met.

And so I booked a flight home. But I made a new vow: to bring Americans back with me – someday – to show them the holy land, *Eretz Hakodesh*, the best place on Earth, and the small part of it that is my wonderful village.

My parents of course met me at airport. My mother was so excited she hugged me with such strength that we both broke into tears. When we arrived at home, there was a very small reception, since it was well known that I could not abide that sort of thing. I've always preferred to keep a low profile. The next day my grandmother came to visit and asked the questions foremost on her mind: "Is there sun in America? Do they have sheep? Are they the same as our sheep?" Everyone was filled with envy and pride when I showed them the pictures I took in America, saying, "I was here, I was there!" I could see that they, too, wished to one day visit America.

In retrospect, my New York City tour seems like a script for a movie – a Bedouin shepherd who finds himself in downtown Manhattan! And it proved to be one of the greatest adventures of my life – like a miracle, and perhaps it was. The shift from my village to the wild, throbbing life of New York City embodies, more than anything, the overlap of different worlds, the split between traditional and modern, conservative and liberal values, a closed society where daily life is totally circumscribed and the independence of contemporary youth which have come to define me as a man, born of one culture, embracing another, all the while trying to straddle them both.

Chapter 3
University, Police Service and Unexpected Opposition

A few weeks after my return from New York City, I started my studies at Haifa University. I always thought I would study something practical that would enable me to work and live near my family and contribute to my community. My original plan was to study agriculture. But now I decided on a political science major: less practical, but it fit my personality and new outlook.

I also wanted to keep my vow to myself to bring Americans to Israel, so with the help of Professor Barry Berger, the director of the overseas students program at Haifa University (to whom I owe the credit for my spoken English as it was the first time in my life I spoke English to a class) I arranged the first trip for foreign students, mostly Americans, to my village. Today, when looking back at it, I realize how it was much more than a "trip." The students spent much of the day, with me acting as expert and guide, hiking along the Tzipori Wadi where they learned not only about the geography and natural history of the area, but also heard stories told by the Bedouin tribes who lived there or who had come this way in years past. The highlight of the day was the amazing meal with my family and the chance to experience real Bedouin hospitality. From the students' feedback, I came to understand that a cross-cultural adventure like that was more of a learning experience for them than any lecture could have ever been. More than a few of these students continued to return to us in the village on their weekends and holidays.

When I think of it, this work with the Overseas Students at Haifa University was my first venture into what I am doing now as a diplomat, only on a much smaller scale. The truth is, I still use my personal experience and perspective to help others understand not only my specific background as an Israeli Bedouin, but also as a representative for Israel. In any event, the students' visit to Khawalid was highly successful and word spread quickly among groups visiting Israel from America. Hundreds, and later thousands, of visitors would visit us to learn about Bedouins in Israel, and the story of one Bedouin in particular who visited America. Once, I met with a group of evangelical Christians from Pennsylvania, and when they asked where in America I had been, I answered Brooklyn. They all laughed, saying that Brooklyn isn't really America. Of course, it's just as American as Pennsylvania. Actually, what surprised me was that many Americans had never even been to New York City.

If at high school I often felt like an outsider, at Haifa University it didn't seem much of an issue. For one thing, there were a number of other Bedouin students, and the atmosphere was more accepting of diversity. It was a relief to feel free to connect with my fellow Bedouins, and also to fit into the life of the university. By this time, I was much more mature than the boy I was at high school. My trip to New York City helped me express my independence and accept my surroundings. But even though I was attending the university in Haifa, I was still very much connected to Khawalid. I commuted almost two hours each direction to college every day, and in the evenings I hitchhiked back to be with my family. The hard part of it all was that there was no privacy to do university work – in that way, home life hadn't changed at all. It was a new challenge every evening, but renting an apartment or living in the dorms was too expensive for either me or my parents. In all honesty, I feel no sense of nostalgia about my university years. It was really hard. Living with my parents was like living in a goldfish bowl, and I worked ten times harder than my friends. At some point, I realized that the key to future success did not lie in what grades I received in my courses, but on the strength of my total knowledge and abilities, and, of course, in the way I would apply those skills. My mother had taught us all to believe in ourselves. I did. And the campus experience solidified that belief.

In the summer of 1994, after completing my college degree, I decided to follow my brother's footsteps into national service. I felt it would be my natural contribution to the well-being of my country. I enlisted in the Israeli police force, and based on my entrance exams, was made a second sergeant. I began my basic training with two other Bedouins. They would become my friends, only to die tragically while on duty a few years later. Both were married and both left loving wives and small children.

After basic training, when we stood to be sworn in, I remember being with filled with pride for reaching this important moment in life. For many in the crowd watching, I would have looked like a Yemenite Jew – a "typical" Israeli. But I wasn't, and when my name was called and it was my turn to be sworn in, I was handed the Koran on which to swear an oath to serve my country, Israel. A few years later, when my brother Maher would be re-living this same experience, I recalled how I had felt on this pivotal day of my life: another chapter in my search for identity and a step toward becoming who I am.

It might seem strange for a Muslim to enlist in the Israeli Army, but Bedouins have historic and political reasons for serving in the Israeli military. I have already mentioned the close relations our grandparents built with the first Jewish pioneers in the 1920s, 30s and 40s. Historically, Bedouins had been mistreated by the Ottoman regime and also by the British regime, and had tensions with the rest of the Arab community. As a result, Bedouins naturally allied themselves with the Jews, who had no animosity toward them, and Bedouin men served both with the Haganah and the Palmach, the pre-state Jewish military organizations that were established to provide security to the Jewish *Yishuv*, the new settlements, towns and cities. When Israel was established in 1948 and military service became mandatory, Bedouins were made exempt from compulsory service until their social and economic situation improved, yet many of us have continued to volunteer to serve. It has become part of our heritage as well.

We all play various roles in life and in these roles our experiences and impressions change the way we see both our external reality and ourselves. My time in the Israeli police provided me with intense and memorable experiences that helped shape my views. Generally, those who serve in the military and police forces – whether in Israel, America, France, or any other democracy – share a bond that is hard for outsiders to understand. We willingly put ourselves in harm's way in service to our nation, and when trouble arises, we focus on the welfare of our comrades, the success of our missions, and on our own survival. In this shared experience, we form a brotherhood and sisterhood that is not translatable or understandable to those who have never served. There's no explaining the dependence and trust soldiers have in one another. It's visceral. It enters the soul. This is what happened to me and to my fellow Bedouin soldiers, and this connects us in an unbreakable bond with our fellow Israelis. Regardless of religion or ethnicity – as soldiers, we step and move together within a shared purpose, fate and destiny. As individuals we may not always agree, but as a unit moving through dangerous terrain, we are brothers, linked inextricably, one to the other.

In uniform during my service with the Israel Defense Force

This is Israel. Each soldier or policeman is a part of Israel, part of the whole, connected to each other through experiences that burn our identity as Israelis into our hearts.

Israel is an immigrant country, an assemblage of cultural groups from all over the world – a multi-ethnic state combining Sephardic and Ashkenazi Jews, Bedouins, Druze, Arabs and more, who coalesce to make the country great. That microcosm, the military, the Israel Defense Force, is the melting pot of it all, a cauldron of cultures. Within this multicultural soup, young men and women are forced to confront stereotypes and prejudices. IDF military training includes education about our shared country and varied cultures of its inhabitants. It is taught in the classroom atmosphere, but it comes alive when multi-ethnic soldiers live, eat and fight shoulder-to-shoulder, sharing the same fate. We get to know each others' backgrounds, customs, and food – a stew of disparate values and ideas, and the end result is a much enhanced effectiveness in the IDF's daily missions. We are compelled to find a common language and common ground, despite our differences. The IDF is truly creating a new Israeli culture, without losing our individual ethnicities. It is difficult to understand such contradictions, but only tiny Israel can put them all together. This is the Israel I love, and that is why these "contradictions" are at the heart of so many of the stories I bring with me when I speak to the world.

After two years as a sergeant in the Israel police, I decided to apply for a graduate degree at Tel Aviv University. I had hoped to continue with the police at least part time while completing my degree, but my request wasn't approved, so I decided to leave the force and continue my education. Thus, in November, 1995, I started my degree in political science with a focus on international relations. It turned out to be the correct choice.

Now, armed with my bachelor's degree from the University of Haifa and a master's from Tel Aviv University, I found a position at the American Embassy in Tel Aviv. First I worked in the information department and later in the consular section. While serving as a translator, I participated in preparations for then President Clinton's historic visit to Israel and Gaza. It was my first exposure to diplomacy. I also took note of the dedication of American diplomats in their efforts to mediate a peace agreement between Israel and the Palestinians. These Americans were committed to serving and representing their country in the best way possible, even though it meant living far away from their homes and families. I became friends with many of them and I heard their stories of serving all over the world. I thought, they are nomads just like me – only

*Receiving my Masters Degree
at Tel Aviv University – 1999*

more so: they wander from country to country and from continent to continent.

By this time I was twenty-nine years old, perhaps young by Western standards, but in the Bedouin world it was considered unusual that I wasn't already married. Every time I spoke to my parents, it seemed they were urging me to get married. I suppose they were like every parent on the planet, only more so! I will forever remember them saying, "We're not going to live forever, and we're not getting any younger. Find a young Bedouin and marry her and build your family." On the one hand I thought getting married would bring me peace of mind, but on the other ... maybe a wife would forever make my mind super busy and not focused on anything! And then again, isn't marriage part of the beauty of life, not just about having a young generation of "Ishmaels," but a true partner who supports and shares one's life experiences?

It was time to think seriously about the future, to consider more long-range plans. Should I return to my family and village? Find a wife, settle down? But what would I do for a living? Go back to the kibbutz factory? Unfortunately, the answer was obvious: I could do nothing more in my village. That path no longer existed for me. This was the bittersweet moment of truth. In opposition to all that my tradition and culture holds dear, my home would have to be wherever my career took me.

But something happened to me in my college years that I haven't yet mentioned – something that also changed the course of my life. Her name is … well, I'll call her S.

She is the eighth of nine children from a small, tribal Bedouin village in the western Galilee. We first met when I attended college with her eldest brother. She was still in high school. When she turned fifteen years old, a marriage to her first cousin was arranged, so of course I never really thought of her as a possible bride. Through my friendship with her brother, I watched her grow up. I became a close friend not only to her, but to her family as well. I should say they were from a different tribe than I, which even today can be a problem. I remember her as a quiet, innocent, girl, with no idea what the future had in store for her, but every time I visited her family, this curious, pretty girl came out to greet me – the young friend of her eldest brother – and always wanted to hear what I had to say. It soon became clear – at least to me – that S and I would be perfect for each other – but it was too late. She was betrothed.

I also knew that her mother wasn't happy with the arrangement for S's marriage, but what could she do? Her father had agreed and given his word. The rest was prescribed by tradition and its rules. I had never imagined that I would fall in love with her, but it happened. And being in love with someone who is "promised" to her first cousin is not easy.

The years came and went, and I visited her family frequently. Step by step, I felt her desire, too, to speak up and talk to me. I saw the excitement in her eyes when we would sit together during my visits. None of this was spoken aloud of course. It was simply understood. At some point her mother sniffed out the story, and, much to my amazement, began inviting me more and more.

In the beginning, I was very cautious. I'd always call and speak with her father or one of her brothers before coming for a visit in order to avoid any possible suspicion. But often when I telephoned, S would answer, and we'd be able to chat. It all was very innocent. But the time came when I no longer could hide my feelings. Finally I told her, "I'm in love with you!"

She blushed with embarrassment, and perhaps something else. But she said, "Ish, I am promised to my cousin, and we're getting married some time next summer. The entire village knows about it, and I don't want to cause any problems. I accept my father's decision."

Her answer tore me up inside. "What should I do now?" I thought to myself. Should I give up and let her go? I knew in my heart of hearts that she felt the same for me, and that her mother would be supportive of our marriage. Again, tradition came between me and my future. It didn't seem right. I thought of my sister, Jamila, who also accepted an arranged marriage to a first cousin. Three months after the birth of her first and only baby, she and her husband separated and later divorced. Today, Jamila lives with my parents and her 13-year-old son, Amir.

I knew then that I would never let go. I would do everything possible, everything needed, no matter how long it would take, to have her as my wife. "Patience, Ish," I said to myself. "Let her grow up a bit and continue to talk with her and her mother." Now this was not easy either. S was already eighteen years old, and at that age she was not permitted to meet a man in person without violating strict Bedouin tradition. I decided it would be okay to continue our chats on the phone from time to time. So I kept calling, filling her in on life in the modern world, not only my life, but the life she could have too: studying, living abroad, seeing the world and meeting new friends. She was confused and hesitant. I accepted this too.

And then, suddenly – her arrangement to her cousin was ended! I jumped at the chance to speak with her father.

Although S's mother knew of my intentions and supported them, I had no idea what her father might think. I held my breath and called him.

There was a silence on the other end, and then in a warm voice he began, "Ish, we know you. My wife already told me and I have no problems with this match. Talk to my daughter. I will support her in whatever she decides."

I was elated! My future happiness was assured.

And then I spoke to S.

She didn't like the idea! Her entire village was gossiping about her, about how she was in love with someone from a different tribe, and right on the heels of her having ended the engagement with her cousin! The tongues were wagging, but I like to think mostly out of jealousy. I had just been accepted into the Foreign Service of Israel and was going to be a diplomat. S's girlfriends would scare her by saying, "Ishmael will be sent to Africa! Is that where you want to go?" I knew what they were telling her and felt desperate. Even were I to promise her the stars and the moon, her girlfriends' words would always be stronger than mine. But I swore I would not give her up. I wouldn't even conceive of the possibility.

But I'm getting ahead of myself. The girls had a point about me. I was indeed a world traveler even before becoming a diplomat. During all this romantic drama, which took place over several years, I had decided to go back to America on my own. I made the decision the moment I realized I could never go back to my old life in the village. I thought: What could be more logical than returning to America? I was more mature now, more educated, and my English was much better. I was ready to take on more challenges in my life, and America seemed more promising than anywhere else. I began to plan my trip to New York, to live the dream of returning to the city I had visited in my youth. However, national politics suddenly took a more central position in my life and delayed my plans.

It was now September 2000, and the Palestinian second Intifada began. My close friend, Ahmad Mzarib, a border police officer, and like me, a Bedouin from the Galilee, was killed at a checkpoint while stopping a car, laden with explosives, from entering Jerusalem. We had met each other during our training just a few years earlier. He left behind a wife and a small child. His death saved the lives of many Israeli citizens. Within another year, yet another dear friend, Samih Sweidan, also a Bedouin border police officer, would suffer the same fate.

In the days after Ahmad's funeral, I pondered what, as a Bedouin, was the right thing for me to do? If Bedouins are an integral part of Israeli society, how else might we express our contribution? In such difficult times, is it only through military or police service, and the looming possibility of death that one could serve one's country?

What role should I play now?

My decision was that I too, have a right to represent my country abroad. I had put my life on the line for my country, and now I wanted to serve it in a political way, as a diplomat. I believed I had the ability and qualifications. I knew, however, that it would take time to be accepted into the diplomatic corps. In the meantime I would once again travel to America – get some experience as a spokesperson for Israel, and do a stint as a citizen diplomat – a completely non-official, people-to-people style of diplomatic activity. I contacted my friends on the East Coast and in Michigan, and arranged to speak on a few college campuses as a start. I planned everything on my own – where to go, how to get there, what to say about Israel. My idea was to explain Israeli society, culture and politics from the perspective of the Bedouin minority in the Jewish State. Of course I was very nervous and excited. This would be my first time in America since those early years. And I sensed it could be the beginning of a whole new career for me, a new purpose to my life, and an adventure in America far more meaningful than the first.

Finally, in October, 2002, I flew into JFK, and took the subway to Brooklyn. What a difference time makes! I had missed Brooklyn so much and wanted to see it once again. This time, I knew where I was, where to go and how to navigate the buses and subways. This was the polar opposite of my experience from my first trip ten years before. The place was the same. It was I who had changed.

After a full day in New York, I took the Greyhound bus to Philadelphia. I wanted to see my friends Pastor Mark Sleinkofer and his wife, Vicki, whom I had met six years earlier in Jerusalem. Mark is a young, devoted evangelical Pastor whose love for Israel amazes me. He and his congregation taught me about the evangelical world and its support for Israel. I had a wonderful visit with Mark and Vicki. We toured Philadelphia and rural Pennsylvania. I will never forget the trip we took to the Adirondack Mountains in northern New York State to attend a Thanksgiving dinner with his mother and extended family. It was a touching experience that connected me to a new portion of American culture and the closeness American families experience on such occasions.

During my stay in Philly, I met Sandy Moskowitz. Sandy worked as a program director for a Jewish community center. Earlier, I had contacted her about a speaking engagement at the center. My story moved her and we quickly became friends. In fact, as Humphrey Bogart said to the French police in *Casablanca*, this was "the beginning of a beautiful friendship!" To put it bluntly, Sandy and her husband, Dr. Barry Moskowitz more or less adopted me! And they remained my adoptive family during all the years I lived in America.

After a week in Pennsylvania with Mark and Vicky, I took the bus to Boston to visit a friend at Harvard. While there, he convinced me to speak to his Jewish student friends. I spoke to them about the situation in Israel and shared my story about being a minority in Israel. Two days before I left Boston, I received an email from Professor Zvi Gitelman at the University of Michigan. Zvi was on a teaching sabbatical at Tel Aviv University, where I took his course on ethnicity and politics. He knew I was coming to Ann Arbor to visit another friend I had met while in Israel. He asked me if I would speak to his class at University of Michigan. I remember him saying, "Don't worry about the English, it will be fine." I agreed! Zvi offered to cover the cost of transportation and the hotel.

Though he mentioned flights, I said I preferred to take the bus. I honestly had no idea how far Ann Arbor was from Boston. The bus trip to Michigan was very long, taking more than a day and a night. It was my first long bus trip and I loved every minute of it. I loved seeing rural America, from the hills and mountains of New York State to the forests of Pennsylvania and the flat fields of Ohio and Indiana. I so much enjoyed the trip that in the years to come I became addicted to traveling by Greyhound. I bussed all over America – from Ogallala, Nebraska to the endless flat fields of Kansas to the corn hills in Iowa! Those bus trips showed me an America I would otherwise never have seen – and for all you who take planes everywhere and really haven't seen your own country – I highly recommend it.

At the University of Michigan, I spoke to professor Gitelman's class and stirred some controversy, mainly due to one Palestinian student. Witnessing anti-Israeli activism on American campuses was an entirely new experience for me. It was the first time I was exposed to the idea that Israel's battlefield during the Intifada was a cause of anti-Israeli feeling. Israel is attacked in the world of public opinion, accused of being also a racist state, an aggressor, and an oppressor. So I decided that the most effective thing to do would be to speak to them about the reality of Israel, what really is happening on the ground, and at the same time share my personal story as a proud, third generation Israeli and a Bedouin. I had served in the Israeli police, and in the Israeli Defense Ministry, and had lost two Bedouin friends, God bless their memory, on duty. In a flash of insight, I realized that my contribution to my country lay in my ability to speak up for it, and so I started a new journey – call it political, call it what you will, but I felt the rightness of it, and I knew it was my time to act. For me, it was a moral imperative.

Because interest in the Palestinian Intifada was so high, and my situation was so unique, I began to receive requests from around the United States to speak and lecture. With the help of Hasbara Fellowships, a student organization based in New York City, I began my new journey of speaking tours that ranged from cities throughout the United States and continued in Canada, Australia, and the United Kingdom. Speaking on college campuses gave me the opportunity to provide students with a rare perspective on Israel. I have a rather unique view of the history and growth of the country, one that is rarely heard, an Israeli who not Jewish, nor a big Zionist. I spoke simply of one man's story within Israel's culture, society, and politics. My ultimate goal was to advocate for Israel and dispel the myriad of erroneous facts that are unfortunately often accepted as truth.

There are so many false accusations made against Israel on campuses around the world, so much bias against Israel, it's hard to fathom. I found only a few pro-Israel activists struggling to counter these lies. And I have to say I didn't come to North America to preach that Israel was perfect. Like every other nation in the world, Israel has its problems. But I was shocked to discover many students who tried to stop me from speaking. In one of the most egregious cases, while addressing the students at Langara College in Vancouver, Canada, the student union tried to ban me from telling my story. Even worse, they had the audacity to compare me to Joseph Goebbels, the Nazi propaganda minister, claiming that I was doing the same for Israel.

America is supposed to be the "land of the free," the

bastion of free speech; the New Hampshire slogan reads, "Live Free or Die." I was stunned that the sentiment against Israel was so strong that some student governments compromised their own dignity and values in an attempt to stifle free speech. It was not only not fair, it was not right.

This deep-seated hatred and these extreme forms of criticism of Israel manifested themselves throughout the country, often in the form of loaded questions posed by anti-Israel students. I found myself in the "eye of the storm," dealing with some heavy political questions. A Muslim student at Rutgers University completely ignored the fact that Israel was a free state with freedom of religion when he asked, "How could you support the Hebrew State if you're not Jewish?" Another student added: "Don't you think that if Israel didn't exist, then the Palestinians wouldn't have any problems?" In Milwaukee someone posed, "How many old Palestinian men and women have you humiliated while serving in the Israeli police?"

As an Israeli who grew up on the fact that Israel is at the heart of the Jewish identity, and that Jews all over the world are committed to its existence, I expected to get support from a large number of Jewish students. Unfortunately, this wasn't the case, and this, too, shocked me. I thought Jews all over the world cared about Israel and its future. Indeed, I was far less shocked by the Arab and anti-Israel questioners than I was with the remarkable apathy of the majority of Jewish students.

I have spoken and met with thousands of students. The reactions I received have taught me much, not only about Israel and its relation with the Jewish Diaspora, but also about my status as a non-Jew representing Israel as a Jewish State.

The last experience for me in those tours was going to speak at U.C. Berkeley. Berkeley is considered one of the most politically vocal places, not only in the United States, but in the entire world. In February 2004, after another long bus tour that had begun in New York City two weeks earlier, I arrived in Berkeley. I had been invited to speak at U.C. Berkeley about the rights of minorities in Israel and the future of the Israel-Palestinian conflict. I had been warned that Berkeley was home to radical ideas when it came to politics and government, and that I should be "careful." People told me, "Good luck, Ish." Still, I wasn't scared; Berkeley and the Bay Area in general is probably one of the most diverse places on the planet. Four years later, in 2008, as an Israeli official in San Francisco, I finally understood what Berkeley is all about.

In conclusion, if you ask me what was I feeling after all of those tours, the answer would be simple – I felt weird. The last thing I expected was to be opposed on American campuses in the way I was. But it reflected something about the atmosphere on American campuses, and how American students think of us, Israel, and how badly one can be treated in "the land of the free, home of the brave." But at the end, I suppose, that is the beauty of democracy.

Chapter 4
An Israeli Diplomat ... and America in My Parents' Eyes

Being a diplomat is no easy task. Being an Israeli diplomat today, for many reasons, is even harder. To make matters more complicated, imagine that the Israeli diplomat is an Israeli Bedouin and a Muslim. I doubt the situation could be more complex.

In October 2004, after two years of roaming the world, traveling to the U.S., Canada, the U.K. and Australia (hey, I am, after all, a nomad) and speaking on behalf of Israel, I joined the Foreign Service and became Israel's first Bedouin diplomat. Those two years of confrontation convinced me of my ability to represent my country, and I decided it was time for me to join forces with the government. Becoming a diplomat in the Ministry of Foreign Affairs was an immense accomplishment for me and signified a breakthrough in Israel in its efforts to integrate Bedouins and other minorities into Israel's Foreign Service. More than anything, I felt that I was reaping the benefits of my parents' investment in me.

After six months of basic training, I was assigned to the Arabic media department, and in July 2005, I was "pushed to the cold water" as Israel's spokesperson on the issue of the disengagement from Gaza – when Israel withdrew eight thousand Israeli citizens from the Gaza Strip. It was an exciting opportunity for me, as I appeared on every Arabic TV station. Even in Israel it was still rather new and unfamiliar to see a Bedouin as Israel's spokesperson, and the Israeli media described me as "Israel's face in the

*Representing Israel in the media to the
Arab world – from the Gaza Strip – 2005*

Arab world."

Preparing to become a diplomat began long before my actual steps toward a professional career. My experiences as a Bedouin in Israel, an ethnic minority in a democratic state, inspired me to seek out exactly these types of cross-cultural and inter-ethnic exchanges that are at the core of making a good diplomat. My strong Bedouin and Israeli values, including deep mutual respect for others, have greatly aided me.

In March 2006, a year and a half after joining the Foreign Service, I was appointed as Deputy Consul General to the U.S. Pacific Northwest, based in San Francisco. Usually, in our Foreign Service, the first assignment is to a "hardship post." Serving as a diplomat in the wonderful San Francisco area might sound like an easy choice, but there is the flip side to consider: it is home to one of the most opinionated populations in the world, with quite a vocal anti-Israel contingent. Of course, I never assumed I would have an easy life, so I welcomed the challenge and off I went to this very interesting "hardship post."

There are huge cultural differences between a Bedouin village, with its highly conservative traditions, and the Bay Area, one of the most open, progressive communities in the world. My two years in the Israeli Consulate in San Francisco has provided me with many stories and is the main reason I wrote this memoir. Aside from my earlier adventures of a young, naive boy, much of what I have experienced while working in my professional capacity has been nothing less than shocking.

Many people frankly questioned how a Bedouin could represent and speak on behalf of the Jewish State of Israel. Others simply asked in disbelief: Does Israel really have non-Jews? Such questions were to be the mainstay of my time in America. I learned early on to always begin by explaining who I am: an Israeli Bedouin and Muslim. This usually piqued people's curiosity, and opened the door to many wonderful conversations.

One of the first tough questions I encountered upon my arrival to San Francisco was this: "Ishmael, you were sent thousands of miles away from home to advocate on behalf of Israel's reputation for equality, civil rights, and democracy. But how do you feel about the fact that back in your home village, among your Bedouin brothers and sisters, you are not entitled to this equality of which you speak?" It was asked by a Jewish woman at a house gathering in Tiburon, a wealthy enclave in Marin County, north of San Francisco, and it not only challenged me as a diplomat, but also renewed that ongoing process of questioning myself about my identity – not merely who I am as a person, but what really is my status and position as a minority in Israel.

My immediate response was that Israel isn't a perfect country and faces many challenges. I also reminded her that America is not perfect either, and America has been working on democracy for several hundred years. Israel, on the other hand, is a relatively new democracy, working through complex citizenship and legal questions. I, as a free man in that democracy, have rights, protections and responsibilities that will enable me to one day help change our society and make it more equitable. Of course, I realized that this is not the entire picture, and the answer is more complex than a simple reassurance that "we will get there someday." I am not naive. I know discrimination in Israel continues to exist. But I feel it is our role, the younger generation's, to dedicate ourselves to the elimination of discrimination and to seek true economic and social justice throughout our society. There are African American diplomats representing the United States – now there is an African American president – but that doesn't mean discrimination does not exist in America, and it also doesn't mean that, because there is discrimination, African Americans should wash their hands of their country of birth. In addition, I am also not blind to the fact, and feel compelled to point out, that we Israeli minorities live better than any of our counterparts throughout the Middle East.

By any measure one chooses, whether educational opportunity, economic development, women's and gay rights, freedom of speech and assembly, or legislative representation, Israel's minorities fare far better than minorities in any other country in the Middle East. The reason is simple: Israel, founded by Jews and including minorities within it, has created the most dynamic, democratic, and hopeful society in the region. This is not because of the practice of Judaism per se. After all, until the establishment of Israel, many Jews lived in the surrounding Arab countries. Rather, it is because Israelis have brought innovation and economic development and Western-style democracy to the region.

Today, Israel is linked to Silicon Valley, Europe, Asia, Australia, and all of the advanced economic regions of the globe. New ideas are continuously helping develop and change our society. On the other hand, we have to acknowledge the role of Jewish teaching and values in the evolution of these cultural innovations: education has always been a top priority for Jewish people no matter where they lived. It is because of Judaism that Israel is what it is today.

By allying ourselves with the Jewish population in Israel, our community has reaped many rewards. Do we receive as many benefits as Jewish citizens? No. Are our schools, roads, infrastructure as well built as those in Jewish neighborhoods? No. Do we have the same employment opportunities as most Israeli Jews? No. However, it needs to be understood, that many of these differences are cultural and Bedouin-specific. Our lifestyle and very conservative heritage is further constrained by tribal rules and customs. This creates a sort of self-imposed barrier to full integration into a modern life.

Despite the government's efforts to do its part in providing educational infrastructure, Bedouins still have difficulty competing with our fellow Israelis from the big Jewish towns and communities. Jewish communities are more organized, while our settlement process had been traditionally spontaneous and unplanned. Our hope had been to build and establish a blueprint for a new era of Bedouin villages and communities, but the reality was not as successful as one might have envisioned it. What use would it be to create a modern villa with a swimming pool, satellite dish, and broadband Internet access for a Bedouin who can only relate to his own culture and customs? Would the change of environment morph someone like my grandmother into a "modern" woman? These changes, while arguably desirable, must and will happen gradually.

I don't have the right merely to elucidate the problems my community has, to complain about discrimination and inequality, and then simply run away. My moral responsibility is to take these differences between my community and the mainstream Jewish population and construct out of them a bridge that connects these communities to each other, so that, shoulder to shoulder, we can work as brothers to make our country a better place for all of us. And the truth is, compared to America and the rest of the Western democracies, Israel has come a long way in its efforts to ensure that citizens of all religions, cultures, and races, are treated equally. On a personal level, I have worked hard to understand the many aspects of my mixed identity and my status as a minority in Israel. And much of that I learned, ironically, while living and working as a diplomat in San Francisco.

My present role as a diplomat is quite different from my former role as a border policeman, and yet there are similarities. I am still serving society, but now the battlefield is rhetorical, not physical. Being a spokesman for Israel is simply another way of defending my country, which is the mission and pleasure of my life.

Interestingly, I came to notice that regardless of the specific issue I was discussing, questions tended to always focus back to one area: blaming one's government, whether Israeli or American. During the Bush II years, I recall one incident when I was explaining my perspective that in general it's wrong to blame the government as the source of all our problems or look to it as the source of all solutions. An elderly woman in the last row stood up and said, "Ish, we're having a good time hating George Bush. Don't take that away from us!" I wanted to burst out laughing. But it was also sad. I wondered why people would waste so much time blaming and criticizing their governments rather than trying to fix the problems themselves and then educate others. It reminded me of something that was told to me years ago by Ezra Shemesh, an Iraqi Jew, who lived in the small Jewish town of Kiryat Ata. He owned a vegetable store and was a good friend to almost everyone in the village who came there to shop. He used to say, "If someone eats a falafel, and a fly falls in it, he will blame the government." Alas, I guess he was right.

Berkeley

All storms have a center. The tumultuous atmosphere of Berkeley is no different. Berkeley is the location where I inevitably encountered the greatest unabashed misrepresentations of Israel and Israeli policy, openly expressed as animosity toward Israel, the effect of which would only deepen the divisions between Israel, the Palestinians, and Israel's neighbors. In June 2007, a year after the "Second Lebanese War" ended, I was invited to participate in a debate with a Lebanese professor for his class in Middle Eastern Studies at U.C. Berkeley. The warnings and alerts that I had received years ago when I first spoke in Berkeley came into play. About eighty students attended the debate. As always, I arrived early to find the location of the class-room. The first hint that challenges lay ahead was when the professor asked those students who had also arrived early whether they were "ready for a fun class?" "Fun class," I asked myself. "What's fun about a debate about the Middle East?" Regardless, I was happy to contribute my experiences to help educate these Berkeley students, and I was delighted to see such a large turnout of students for Middle East studies, thirsty to hear about the region from a first-hand source. I was in for a great shock and disappointment. Instead of an informative and interesting debate, I found myself arguing with a professor whose sole purpose was to attack Israel, without even offering even one alternative as to what might be done to change the situation. The saddest part was that the professor of this esteemed university would not even shake my hand, nor did he ever refer to me, or Israel, by name. Instead of being a constructive event, beneficial to the students, the debate turned into a confrontational bashing of Israel and me.

I looked into the students' eyes, and I could see that even many of them were surprised at his behavior. I explained that, first of all, when we speak about the Middle East, we speak of a region that both the professor and I came from, a place where mutual respect and hospitality are an important part of the culture. I had expected that culture to extend to this classroom – in as much as I was a guest of the class. If we do not even fulfill that, then what are we teaching our students? What message we are sending? What good can come from such a "debate?" I told the students that this sort of exchange allows us only to wallow in shared mud, without any hope of progress, and that this is exactly what is happening today in Arab countries in the Middle East who are mired in the past, instead of looking for channels of understanding that will lead them to the future and help them reach a solution to the conflict with Israel.

When I spoke of the extent of Israel's accomplishments, especially in science and technology, after only sixty short years of independence, I asked, as an aside, how many years of statehood will America be celebrating next July 4th? The students looked at each other in total confusion. They simply didn't know! Did I change any of their minds about Israel? About the way we need to discuss these issues in an open and respectful way? About learning for themselves the facts and not just listening to propaganda? I don't know. In the end, we had a friendly conversation and I promised to return and speak to them again if they were to invite me. Alas, that invitation never came.

First launched in Toronto, in 2005, the first week in March has been designated Israel Apartheid Week by activists who seem either ill-intentioned or misinformed. On American and Canadian campuses organizing committees plan events intended to castigate Israel and portray Israel as the cause of all Middle East unrest.

In 2008, I had the opportunity to "dialogue" with some of the organizers of these events at U.C. Berkeley. My perspective is unique, both as Vice Consul for Israel in San Francisco and, not only as a Bedouin, but also the highest-ranking Muslim representing Israel in the United States. My very existence proves that Israel is one of the most culturally diverse societies and the only true democracy in the Middle East.

Being a diplomat and representative of a country

that I love is a great joy, yet it brings with it definite frustrations. Words must always be couched in the language of diplomacy. Remarks cannot be accusatory; they must be respectful and carefully chosen so as to keep all doors of communication open. And yet, there are times when I would like to shed these restrictions and speak of the contentious subjects with the clarity in which I see them – as Ish the Bedouin-Israeli rather than Ish the Diplomat. I suppose I would be too blatantly direct, saying, "You are part of the problem, not part of the solution. If you are truly committed to a better world, please end the false, inflammatory rhetoric. We need moderate people to come together in good faith to help find the path to relieve human suffering on both sides of the Israel-Palestinian conflict. Vilification and false labeling is a blind, unjust path that leads nowhere." But of course as long as I'm a diplomat I guess I'll have to continue to be diplomatic!

The organizers of Israel Apartheid Week are committed to singling Israel out as the source of all problems in the Middle East, a racist and intolerant colonialist imposter with no right to sovereignty, a scourge of the earth. These people go to great lengths to continuously attack not only Israel, but America, including its military, in ways I can scarcely understand. They enjoy the protection and security America provides, yet disdain the government, military, and police who make them safe. They deny Israel the fundamental right every society has of defending itself. They condemn Israel for building a security barrier to protect its citizens from suicide bombers and for striking at buildings from which missiles are launched at its cities. But they never offer an alternative. Aren't they themselves practicing a deep form of racism by denying an entire society the right to defend itself?

Their criticism is willfully hypocritical. Do Israel's Arab citizens suffer from disadvantages? Yes, they do. Do African Americans and other minorities living ten minutes from the Berkeley campus suffer from disadvantages? The answer is also an emphatic, "yes." So should we launch a Berkeley Apartheid Week? Or, should we seek real ways to better our societies and make opportunities available to more people?

Furthermore, and perhaps even more importantly, these activists are betraying the moderate Arabs and Jews everywhere who are working to achieve peace. Their radicalism, in Berkeley and beyond, actually undermines the forces for peace in Israel and in the Palestinian territories. Israel is working hard to achieve a peace agreement that recognizes the legitimate rights of both Israel and the Palestinian people. Many Palestinians are doing the same. And yet these hate groups chip away at our accomplishments by falsely, and foolishly, vilifying one side. If Israel were an apartheid state, I would not have been appointed Vice Consul, and more to the point, I, for one, would *never* have chosen to take upon myself this duty to represent Israel this way. Many Arabs, both within Israel and in the Palestinian territories, have exhibited great courage to walk the path of peace. We welcome everyone to stand with us rather than against us.

The anti-Israeli attitudes in the Bay Area are extremely challenging both for me and my fellow Israeli representatives. Many people hate everything about the Israeli government and Israeli-American relations. I have, at times, felt as though I were thrown into a lion's den, constantly having to defend myself and what I represent, always hoping for a warm and welcoming crowd, but rarely finding one. The attacks have come not only from

the anti-Israeli movement on campuses and in community organizations, but surprisingly, also from the Jewish
community. Questions directed towards me have always
been tough and frequently contain within them extreme
accusations. Only my belief in my duty has helped me
remain persistent in the midst of such hostility.

Still, I wonder why is there such opposition and confrontation in the Bay Area? What breeds such enmity? To
be fair, the mindset in Berkeley seems quite different from
that of the rest of America. Perhaps it is because many
of the people came from the East Coast or the Midwest
seeking a refuge from the "establishment" which perhaps
they identify with in their families and parents. On the
other hand, they came to Berkeley looking for freedom,
love, and peace. Subsequently, a culture of individual
development, personal growth, justice and liberalism has
developed here. Why this leads to hatred of Israel, which
has the same values, is a mystery. And honestly, I believe
that, when you look at the whole picture, even though
we didn't agree with each other on many issues, the Bay
Area's passionate social justice discourse is a remarkable
contribution to democracy.

It wasn't surprising that an Israeli diplomat was not
greeted with any particular warmth, but, it was extremely
difficult to face the rage I encountered on the Arab side
and the ignorance on the Jewish side – all of which com-
pounded my feelings of isolation. After all, I was a stranger
in this country, not living with any family, and someone
who was difficult for people to label – neither fish nor fowl.
Israeli, but not Arab nor Jew.

No diplomat from any other country has had to deal
with the same daily issues as those of my fellow Israeli
diplomats and myself. No country elicits such passion-

filled reactions as does Israel. And, here in America, we have advocates who dedicate time, resources, and talent in ways that are unimaginable for other countries. Israelis may not fully know or appreciate the depth of feeling and the efforts of those Americans – Jews and Gentiles – who are committed to Israel's existence and welfare.

My position as deputy consul is seen by some as a political move by the Israeli government to refute the criticism that non-Jews possess few, if any, opportunities to gain influential roles in Jewish society. Arab students and leftist activists have labeled me as a "Token Bedouin" and an "Uncle Tom." But I did not come to America merely to paint a rosy picture of Israel. Israel is and will always be a Jewish State. It has problems which I readily acknowledge. But it also has strengths, the most important of which is its attempt to provide equality and freedom to all its citizens regardless of their backgrounds.

All this has taught me a great deal about the limits of understanding. I must admit, though, that despite the attacks on me and against Israel, I felt great warmth and regard for the people I met and worked with during my twenty-eight months in the Bay Area. It is a great place, where in addition to cutting edge technologies and medical breakthroughs that were launched here and spread all over America and the world, the community strongly supports social causes: civil rights, women's rights, gay rights, and environmental awareness. While I might not have agreed with all the controversial and confrontational positions that were passionately argued to me, I did not doubt the sincerity and commitment of the advocates who take their activism seriously. They believe they are helping to change the world and make it a better place. This is what makes a healthy democracy and we all should salute those efforts, even of those who oppose our own views.

Even among this ocean of "anti" movements, there were the warm corners, largely unfamiliar to the mainstream Bay Area population and the general California population. I always believed that I had to focus my efforts on the small communities in remote places. As one who came from and grew up in a small place (I used to call it middle of nowhere in Israel!), I felt that many living in the lesser-known places would want the opportunity to hear from an Israeli representative. If Israel is a major part of America's foreign policy, and they hear of us every day in the evening news – then shouldn't America's smaller communities get their information first-hand too? That's why I decided to visit small towns in my jurisdiction as frequently as possible.

When I first moved to San Francisco, the person I most wanted to meet was the local Chabad Rabbi! Chabad is the Jewish organization that focuses on Jewish roots, identity, tradition, and heritage. There are more than four thousand full-time Chabad rabbis who reach out to their fellow Jews in more than three thousand locations worldwide. They work as "unofficial diplomats" in spreading their mission, but they are open, patient, and welcoming to every human being. Always ready to help whenever needed – they provided food to victims during the huge fire in southern California – just one example among many of the assistances they offer.

My first "work" encounter with a Chabad rabbi was back in Buffalo, New York, in 2003 when I met the Gurary brothers, both of whom are rabbis. A pro-Israeli student activist at the University of Syracuse invited me to speak during Purim; however, they were unable to pay for my airfare. Within a day he wrote, "Ish, problem solved!

Speaking at Chabad Buffalo – 2003

Chabad House here would love to host you and co-sponsor this." This was just the sort of hospitality that I, as a Bedouin, had grown up with!

My second encounter was in July 2006, a few months before I left for San Francisco. It was during the second Lebanon war and Chabad representatives arrived, under rocket fire, to my Bedouin village, knocking on people's doors and asking people to let them know what they needed. This can happen only in Israel – very moving.

So during my stay in San Francisco, I was quick to seek out Chabad, and I enjoyed the friendship of Yosef Langer. Rabbi Langer is a large, white-bearded man in his mid-sixties who is the epitome of kindness: warm, human, and welcoming and smiling all the time. Rabbi Langer is very well known in San Francisco, a friend to mayors, actors, politicians, businessmen and women, community leaders, rabbis and pastors. He and his wife, Hinda, have an open house for anyone who wants to come by and learn about Judaism and Jewish values and tradition. There is something special about Rabbi Langer. Our friendship began the moment we met. He has remained close to me whether times were happy or sad, exciting or lonely, stressful or relaxed. He is always on call for me, always available should I need him. These people have values that a visitor cherishes in a strange country, especially when he or she is alone – all alone. Over the course of

With Rabbi Yosef Langer (L) and Dick Berman (R)
San Francisco – 2009

a year we struggled together through many of my issues. We came to trust, respect, and count on each other. In many cases, I would be the one who, on Friday night and *Shabbat*, would deliver kosher food cooked in his house to Jews who were hospitalized, and I did it proudly! In addition to our close association and friendship, Yosef has been an example to me of Jewish values. As such he has given me a great gift of understanding. The best times I ever had in San Francisco were at *Shabbat* dinners at his house. To my friend Rabbi Yosef Langer, I will always be grateful.

This sentiment of gratitude is also held for those in the Evangelical Christian community. Evangelicals are some of the staunchest supporters of Israel: spiritually, politically, and economically. They support Israel because they believe that the words of Moses and the ancient prophets of Israel were inspired by God. They believe that God ordained the emergence of Israel as the Jewish State, in the land promised by God to Abraham, Isaac, and Jacob. They believe that God has a plan for this nation – that He intends it to be a blessing to all the nations of the earth.

Knowing that there are so many Christians in America standing up for Israel gives me great comfort after enduring all the harsh attacks of my first two years. Their support for Israel is significant. They are not a small community in one region of America, but number in the tens of millions. Precisely in these crucial times, as Israel continues to fight for its right to exist, I am grateful to them for not having turned their backs on us.

In January 2009, I encountered one of the strangest situations during the two years stationed in San Francisco. "Operation Cast Lead" was going forward in Gaza, and the consulate received hundreds of emails of both support and protest from all over the region. When the operation ended, I took another look at the emails and geographically mapped the opinions expressed. I communicated with the writers and decided to get out into the field to speak with them directly.

Amazingly, I found myself on a Sunday morning speaking on behalf of Israel before the Evangelical community of Redding, California. There I was, an Israeli Bedouin Muslim, speaking about a Jewish State in front of 250 Christians. I cannot describe the excitement in their eyes or my own warm feelings after having spent so many tense, difficult, long months in the Bay Area. In that church in Redding, located in the northern edge of California's huge Central Valley and worlds away from my homeland, I learned that Israel has many true friends. It was stunning to suddenly be in this situation, in which the entire audience stood and applauded at every sentence I uttered. I could not believe it. We had a shared, unconditional love for Israel.

Until that day, aside from my friendship with Mark Sleinkofer, a devoted Evangelical pastor and Israel supporter whom I had met years earlier in Israel, I had had no interaction with this pro-Israel community. As soon as I began to talk with them, I found myself feeling so much closer to home. They shared the values – mainly social and family values – which I had grown up with. No longer was I provoking major arguments, an experience that consumed me in San Francisco. Beyond the views that the evangelical community and I held in common, I deeply appreciated their commitment to social welfare causes such as feeding the hungry, helping the sick, and giving clothes to the needy – exactly the kind of social morals I was taught by my parents since childhood. Even when we had nothing, our priority was to help others.

Young Americans are highly media-savvy, yet their view of world events is myopic, at best, and often limited to the sound bites they glean from radio, television and the Internet. For all their education and smarts, most young Americans can talk more accurately about the latest movie coming out of Hollywood than they can about the most important world events. They're equipped with laptops, iPods and iPhones and every technological gadget possible. But how do they use them? This, of course, is worlds apart from what I remember of my life at their age. It makes me laugh to recall the huge technological leap we all experienced when the first color television came into our village. Aside from the marvels of viewing shows in color, we had the added bliss of a remote control. My father would walk past us and tap our heads, telling us that we didn't even have to stand up to change the channel. Just point and click. Was that a luxury! Or are all these advances just giving ourselves over to laziness? Why is it that such bright kids in ninth or tenth grade are totally Internet-savvy, yet when you ask them a simple question about America or its neighbors, Mexico or Canada, they are unable to answer? If you ask them where Bismarck, North Dakota is, they might not even be able to find the state on the map. I don't know what the source of the problem is. I can only say that young people's knowledge is horribly inadequate beyond the lure of electronic and computer innovations. This concerns me greatly as I consider the future diplomatic relationship between Israel and the United States. I know that our relationship is viable. But I worry about the knowledge gap of young Americans. How can they possibly make intelligent decisions about international affairs when they are ignorant about what transpires within their own borders? And if their knowledge is derived solely from what they glean in the media, they are limiting themselves to second-hand, biased information.

You might question what were the other aspects of my experience? What was I learning during my time here in America? Here I was, dedicating myself to sharing my experience and knowledge with strangers, and trying to overcome roadblocks of ignorance by providing the community with something that might elevate their awareness and understanding. It was clear that this was my mission. Yet it is very difficult to continue to do this at a steady pace when you are doing it completely on your own, far from the people, family, and culture that are at your very core and source of reference. For me, the saddest times were Fridays, when everyone else was going home to their families for the weekend. Returning to my apartment alone after a maddening week and seeing just the four walls was very difficult – this loneness was extremely hard. You see, Bedouin culture is very open. No invitations are needed to visit. We welcome and indulge our guests. Yet I found that here in America, you needed to make a plan, make a date, R.S.V.P. in advance. How odd, strange, and alienating. Only with my friends at Chabad did I feel that I was welcome at any time.

By this time, the woman I wanted to marry, S, had completed two years of civil service teaching Bedouin and Jewish school children, and now she was attending college. From my faraway station in San Francisco I would call her long distance – me in America, and she in her village in the Galilee – and we would continue our conversation – *the* conversation. I loved her and didn't want her to slip away. As they say, time makes itself, and after more than two years of separation, she began to insert little questions into our talks: What will I do for work in America? How often can I visit my family in Israel? These were all fair questions, but they also meant she was seriously considering my offer. I fully realized that taking a village girl from the Galilee to an apartment in San Francisco was almost *mission impossible.* So I explained and explained, never losing hope. Until at last she agreed.

But of course that wasn't the end of the story. I always thought it would be easy to get married to a Bedouin, and only a Bedouin, and live together and raise a family in an open world. But the reality was far from simple. Bedouins historically pay a bride price to the betrothed and her family, so that in case the couple separates, or something happens to the man, the woman can continue her life independently. In the past, people used to offer camels, which were worth a great deal; later, people paid gold or even land registered in the woman's name. A house wasn't an issue since people lived in tents. But today, when people are more settled and living more modern lives, the house has become the basic prerequisite for any young man who wants to get married. A woman can't leave her parents' house unless a husband provides her with a house of her own.

And I, of course, did not (and as of this writing still do not) have a house! Most of my adult life, I have been away from the village, so consequently I didn't build my own house, as most of the young men do. Instead, I invested all my money and time in my career and education; and as I look back at what I've done in my life, I have to conclude I did the right thing – but the sacrifice has been enormous. As a government employee, it is very difficult to save a lot of money, and it would be extremely untraditional and in fact unacceptable, to acquire a mortgage like the average Israeli or American would do. So that meant I was stuck. No house? No wife! You can imagine how I must have felt – knowing she was ready to say yes, but I couldn't conclude the engagement because I couldn't afford a house for cash, and at the same time couldn't go back to the simple village life.

It was a sad time for me. But as always, I refused to give up. In the meantime I continued my work in the San Francisco consulate.

I'd like to share with you a few of my observations as a foreigner and as a diplomat with regard to American life and politics.

On a personal level, I came to understand, deep under my skin, how lonely American culture can be. It's not very easy to find the kind of intimate friends one can rely on and ask advice of in times of trouble. At first I thought that perhaps I was being too harsh, contrasting America to the kind of tribal family structure that provides cohesive ties among family members such as I grew up with, but I think I was right. Americans are always busy, and when I would call my friends they would ask if I could call after the mid-week or on the weekends so that we could schedule a time for lunch, dinner, or even just a quick coffee. Does one have to wait until the weekend to see one another? To have a chat or get some advice? People in the States live life at a frantic pace – checking emails and answering phones even during lunch or walking on the street or running to the train. I find being a slave to one's Blackberry insane. If the joke goes that Israelis speak on two cell phones at the same time, then I say that Americans hold the entire office in their hands. This is the reason why, unlike other diplomatic colleagues, I always preferred the simple phone to dial and answer calls. People are slow to socialize unless they feel a real need or have good reason. Their careers are more important to them than people. And today, with social network websites such as Facebook, who needs company or friends that might waste your time when you can chat with them from the comfort of your own living room?

Even so, I managed to survive the social isolation. All I had to do was remind myself of the reason why I was there – the State of Israel needed me. The People of Israel look to us in the diplomatic corps with high expectations – and we must meet them. My desire to keep going was bolstered by the hope that I would make a difference, but the thing that really kept me going were my daily talks and text messages with S, the beautiful Bedouin woman with whom I knew I would build my future.

America in My Parents' Eyes

I long dreamed of paying my parents back for all they did to raise me and my siblings. Their hard work and sacrifice allowed me to become the person I am today, and I always think of them whenever success comes my way.

And if my success is theirs, then it was only logical that I would bring them to America to see for themselves what I was doing here and what my love affair with America was all about. When I told them I was bringing them here, they were overwhelmed with excitement. Leaving the village and flying across the ocean to America – just like I did. They were coming to America and would witness its culture and society firsthand. This was quite a trek for a couple who had never been abroad and had rarely seen anything outside their village. Of course, it wouldn't be quite the same for them as it was for me when I made my first trip to this country (no running across live subway rails, for instance!), but I wanted to observe for myself what happens when East meets West, tradition meets modernity, and tribal values and mores meet open democratic principles.

When I proposed the idea of traveling here, my mother immediately and excitedly agreed. She has eighteen grandchildren, a veritable battalion who run around each weekend raising a tumult wherever they go. She lovingly scolds them saying, "It was enough for me to raise your parents, now you?" Coming to America would be a well-earned respite for her. However, it took me months to convince my father. He was fearful as to how he would be received by people in the States, since he did not speak English and could not communicate. He didn't know much about American hospitality in general. Nevertheless, he eventually relented and the journey was afoot.

I flew from San Francisco to Newark International Airport to meet them on their arrival in June, 2007. My plan was to take them to the airport hotel so they could rest and freshen up, and then drive to New York City. I was mischievous enough to want them to have the same tour I had when I first came to Brooklyn seventeen years earlier. I wanted to show them what America is all about, and the first part of that is New York City, America's gateway to the world. And most of all, I wanted to show them Brooklyn and Borough Park. I was so excited about it. Here I was, connecting two totally different cultures, but this time with my parents. I imagined what they would feel and say, anticipating their excitement, especially my father's. He is an intensely curious man, whose sense of adventure opened this new world to me and made it possible for me to get here, even though he himself had never seen it. I wanted to share everything with him and my mother, and I was nervous as to what their reaction would be.

When they landed, they were, of course, extremely excited and happy to see me after an absence of almost six months. But they were exhausted after their twelve hour flight across the ocean. Not easy for them: they were in their early sixties. After heartfelt greetings, my father protested a bit sheepishly, "Ish, I want to sleep." My mother smiled and said, "He wants to smoke as well." Like most Bedouins, my father loves to smoke his homemade cigarettes, and loves his coffee, too. I thought about how lucky they were to have each other, so they never had to be alone or to feel lost, as I had felt when I first arrived in New York. My first experiences in this country were so complicated and convoluted. I suppose it's what every new immigrant or visitor arriving in a strange place goes through if there's no one to take care of him. We say it's like swimming in dark water. Or, as my father told me two days later when we were running around in the airport before our flight to San Francisco, marveling at the huge crowds, "I feel like a cat in the bushes. Or like a poisoned mouse," two phrases we use to describe a confused or lost person. I knew exactly what he meant!

On that first day through, I quickly realized that my planned tour of New York would be too overwhelming for him, so I decided to tackle a small city first. I called my close friend, Sandy Moskowitz in Wayne, Pennsylvania, and told her that we were coming directly to her house. Sandy gave me the directions and we hit the road.

Wayne is about twenty-five minutes outside of Philadelphia. On the day we arrived, it was raining, and instead of sleeping, my parents were like children in a toy store, looking excitedly out at the cars and trees and green lawns all along the way. That lush greenery was their first impression of America, and that vision has remained with them ever since. A month later, when they returned to the village, they could not stop raving about two things: how green and beautiful America is and how hospitable its people are.

Upon arriving at Barry and Sandy's home, my parents needed to sleep, but not before they quickly ate the breakfast Sandy had made for them (their first real taste of American hospitality). My father and Sandy shed some tears as they hugged each other, she knowing him as the father who raised me, and he knowing her as the one who became a surrogate parent for his son when he traveled so far away from his home. What is humanity, if not this? Two worlds away from each other, different religions, cultures, and languages, sitting at a table in a house in a distant land, sharing the most precious thing of all, a child. The Moskowitzs are my role models and example of how the entire world should look. It is not about politics, religion, or anything like that – it's about our shared humanity.

Directly after breakfast, exhaustion and the emotions of the day hit my parents with full force. They slept from noon until almost midnight, losing their sense of time. My mother woke up first, saying, "Ish, why are you up so early?" It was around 11:30 p.m. Sandy and I just laughed. An hour later, my father arose from his exhaustion with a slight sense of disorientation and asked, "What am I doing here? Is this a hotel or a hospital?"

Coming to America for the first time has a tremendous impact on visitors. It is, in my eyes, the best investment America can make: bring young leaders here from all over the globe so they can learn about American values and return home to spread them, thereby gaining more supporters around the world. As with my preconceived notions about America years earlier, my parents' ideas of America were also rooted in the images that were brought to us via the media: milk and gold, a rich country, but also frightening, big, and peppered with undesirables – which, by the way, are also present in every other culture.

The next morning, we traveled to Washington, D.C. Our first visit in this gleaming white city was to the Senate Building to meet with our friend, the U.S. Senator from Minnesota, Amy Klobuchar. I had met her in Israel a few years before. In the afternoon, we took a tour of the Capitol Building with other friends I had met on earlier travels to the East Coast. Although my parents were still tired and trying to cope with a deep case of jetlag, they were

My parents at Starbucks in Washington, D.C.

very excited to see everything they had only glimpsed on TV. This was a new reality. Our tour was amazing, and left a huge impression on my parents. I reminded them that here, in this very place, major decisions that change the world are being made every day.

Perhaps the most touching part of our time in D.C. was the visit to the Holocaust museum. I noticed a lot of anger on my father's face when he saw the pictures – the horror that remains as evidence to the world of the ghettos and Nazi concentration camps. I knew he was recalling the connections we Bedouins had made with the families who arrived in Israel after the war in the years before Israel was established.

We drove back to Philadelphia through the Amish country. Nature, rivers and creeks, mountains and hills, and livestock made my parents feel at home. It reminded them of the open pastoral spaces of northern Israel in which they had grown up. I thought of the wonderful comparison that could be made of my parents' culture with the Amish people in this unique part of America. The rolling, green hills represents a real picture of America as well. Life in America is not just about cities such as New York City and Washington. Driving through the cornfields of Lancaster, Pennsylvania, seeing the Amish with their horse-drawn buggies and distinct and simple clothes – which clearly mark theirs as a culture outside mainstream America – was a thrilling experience. My parents' excitement knew no bounds. After discussing this with each other in their own, wonderfully familiar punctuated Bedouin slang, they asked me whether they could live there, amongst the beautiful farms of the countryside. What a surprise! Only three days in the U.S., and they were already talking about moving here.

From the Amish country we headed north. As we were approaching New York City and I was explaining to them what we were about to see, the magnificent New York City skyline and the Statue of Liberty came into view. They became more and more excited as we crossed the Hudson, but their feelings changed as we entered Manhattan. It was so very noisy, so very crowded and so busy. Skyscrapers to the right and left! My mother said, "Ish, is this now New York?" I repeatedly assured her it was, explaining that it is my favorite city in America. They couldn't believe what they were seeing. When we started walking, after a stop in the hotel, they asked, "How does one see the sun here?" It was frightening to them. Because of that, we went to sleep very early.

The next morning, after their morning prayers, we drove to the U.N. Plaza. They were impressed with the line of photos showing the former secretary generals of the U.N., which for so many of us is the emblem of hope for international peace. From the U.N., we went to the craterous remains of Ground Zero. My father stared in silence, trying to understand it, trying to find an explanation for what was before him. I tried to explain to him what it was he was seeing. A look of anguish mixed with sadness filled his face. My mother, listening to my explanations, kept repeating, "God bless their memory, and God pray for the families left behind." Later on, after we had left the site and were preparing to go to the airport for our flight to San Francisco, my father looked at me and said, "Ish, I read the Koran entirely, and I have no idea how this was done in the name of Islam. The problem is that this blind ideology of hatred gets different interpretations in each place." He continued by saying that when religion is mixed with political aspiration, it is a recipe for failure, trouble, chaos, and bloody conflict. Politics, he declared, must not mix with religion. More than any other thing my parents experienced during their trip here, that scene of utter devastation would become fixed in their minds. The horrors of the terror attacks have brought so many people around the world closer to Americans. It certainly did with my parents.

After a few more days on the east coast, we headed to the west coast.

Our visit to California in general and San Francisco was very different, and gave my parents a whiff of home. The weather (though it was cold for June), the surrounding mountains and hills and the many farms they saw reminded them of their village on the hills in the Galilee. My father repeatedly mentioned how, as a child he was told that when it's daylight in Israel, it's nighttime in America, and that when the sun sets, it rises over America. He was always amazed by that idea, believing that it was magic. As their visit continued, he continued to ask what time it was in Israel and whenever possible, he asked to call family back home just to tell them how different the time was in San Francisco.

I drove them around the city, showing them how lovely, beautiful, diverse, and multicultural the city is. As we drove through a rough San Francisco neighborhood known as the "Tenderloin," my father looked out at the homeless people on the streets. Some lay asleep on the sidewalk while others pushed carts filled with all their worldly belongings. "Stop, stop!" he shouted. He wanted to understand what he was seeing. "What are those people doing? What's happening? Do they belong to San Francisco? Are those people from Sudan?" (At that time, Sudan and Darfur were in the news daily.)

"No," I told him. "They're from here in America, just like many other Americans." But he couldn't comprehend why they were in this terrible situation. Where are their families, he wanted to know? Where is the welfare system or health department? I explained that this is one of the painful realities about America; some of the homeless have families that have abandoned them, some have just fled to the streets, some have drug problems and some are mentally ill, and more. It is not as if Israel is devoid of homeless people. In fact, woefully, their numbers have increased in the last decade, but obviously not nearly to the extent of San Francisco. Our vision of America was always of unending plenty, but this was the exact opposite. My father was shocked. Then he said something I will always remember: "Why, if America and Americans feed the entire world and help countries establish values around the globe, can't they feed their fellow Americans?"

"Can you help them, Ish?" my mother asked.

Her question made me laugh. After all, I was part of a foreign government here, and there's so much help needed back in Israel, especially within my own community. But I said, "I will try," and I think that my heart was true, even though I knew there was very little I could do.

After a long and wondrous month, my parents flew back home to Israel. They returned with many good stories and strong impressions, and came to realize that America is a normal country just like every other. It has poverty and wealth, new and old cities, intelligent minds and woeful ignorance. But more than anything, it was the human touch – meeting wonderful people and experiencing the warm hospitality that people showed them in America – that gave them the longest-lasting stories, stories they have not stopped repeating since they arrived back home. America, just as it happened to me after my first trip, conquered their hearts!

Chapter 5

Israel and America: A Comparison

America is a nation with a civil contract between its people and government, and American identity provides equal privileges. If you ask Americans who they are, they will say "I am an *American*, citizen of the greatest nation on earth." They identify first as foremost as Americans, and only secondarily as Italian-American or Chinese-American or Hindu-American. America is the melting pot *par excellence*. Americans are proud of their country. They tend to believe their system is the best, and if only the rest of the world would adopt their ways, everything would be so much better. It is a good system, but while it's true it works in America, particularly the idea of the melting pot, it does not work that well for Israel, at least not yet.

Countries in the Middle East, including Israel, were formed on a different basis. There are nations and there are groups of mixed ethnic minorities, with different origins, religions, and cultures, and the two do not exactly match. Let's use the food simile of an American soup and see how it works in the Middle East.

If America is a soup, then Israel is a salad. A cucumber is still a cucumber and a tomato is still a tomato even if they are on the same plate and covered by the same dressing. An Israeli Jew is a Jew, an Israeli Bedouin is a Bedouin, and an Israeli Druze is a Druze. They are all ingredients of the Israeli salad. We are a country with "cucumbers" and "carrots" and "potatoes" and together we eat the dish as a soup. On the other hand, the soup is also the sum of its components and is identified as "vegetable soup" because of the mix. Our aim in Israel is not to make everyone "identical" – some sort of generic "Israeli" wearing the same costume, eating the same cuisine, having the same religious beliefs, or even speaking the same language at home. We are learning to respect these differences, to see them as our strength. Indeed, we've made significant progress in this arena, but not enough ... and in my view, this is one of our most important national goals.

Israel is also built on a civil contract between the peoples of the society, but different from America. Our contract is with our varying ethnic groups, not with individuals. Israel was founded and defined as a Jewish State with the rights of all peoples protected. My rights as an individual Bedouin citizen, for instance. The Jewish people have a different set of privileges built into the national contract than do Israel's minorities. As a Bedouin, I have certain rights and obligations (such as serving in the military), but the Bedouin do not have some of same privileges as Jews, such as the right of return which grants automatic citizenship with special economic and status benefits.

We aspire to be like America in democracy, freedom, and equal rights, but we are also like Lebanon in the allocation of privileges. In America, what makes you an American isn't whether you are Christian or what your heritage or ethnicity is. You are all American. Part of this is because in America, there is separation of church and state. In Israel, civic rights such as education, marriage, and burial are based on religious affiliation. There are different sets of principles that evolve into rules for each group.

Israel's Declaration of Independence guarantees equal rights to all its citizens, yet the purpose of the State was to fulfill the dream of the Jewish people. The paradox of these two contradictory yet foundational principles has not been not lost. Israel has been besieged by external threats from Arab countries while Arabs also live as a significant minority population within its borders.

The concept of recognizing Israel as a "Jewish State" has recently taken on added political importance in the search for peace in the region. In my opinion, an updated discussion on the concept of Israel as a "Jewish State" would be helpful. Most people use the term "Jewish State" in a reflexive manner and without deep thought about what that means. Ask the typical person on the street what a "Jewish State" means, and most, even politicians, will give some sort of general and shallow textbook reply. Most talk about the Jewish State in terms of "survival" of the Jewish people. But frankly, in my eyes at least, if all there is to Israel as a Jewish State is as a repository for "Jewish Genes", then there is no point. There must be more to the concept of a Jewish State than survival of Jewish genes for the sake of survival alone. I think the concept of Jewish State includes survival, but not only of physical survival. Rather, the concept deals with spiritual, ethical and social values, interpersonal concepts, social structure, personal commitment, shared history, culture, and much more.

Just as the struggle for human rights and social justice persists in the United States, Israel's march toward full equality for all citizens is a slow, continual process. Even during times of relative peace, it has been very difficult to make the rights of ethnic minorities a serious government priority. The reality is complicated, but it is my belief that the existence of a Jewish State in the Middle East can be a blessing for its minorities, and eventually for the region as a whole, if only we can work together.

Israel can be an example to the entire region. It is the only democratic government in the Middle East that grants full rights to every group (although it may not be as perfect as in older democratic Western societies) as well as freedom of religious practice. For ethnic minorities, Israel is a bridge of understanding and a channel for cooperation between Jews and Arabs that can pave the way for understanding between the Jewish State and the Arab countries surrounding it. In many ways, we share the same culture, religions, and customs. In terms of benefit to the world at large, Israel is an oasis for cutting-edge technological innovation, ground-breaking medical achievements, environmental advancement, and water technology, all of which are great advancements for humanity. The interconnectivity of our global economy, of which Israel is so much a part, facilitates the creation of regional wealth and development. Economic opportunity and reward for effort bring hope for many to better their circumstances and engage their energies in positive endeavors that benefit themselves and society. The opposite is also true. If there is no work, there is no hope.

When most people think of San Francisco, they think of the Golden Gate Bridge, cable cars and the Fisherman's Wharf. Less apparent to the eye, however, is one of the most innovative, wealth-creating, and dynamic centers not only of the San Francisco region, but of the entire world: Silicon Valley. In Silicon Valley, the greatest minds on earth collaborate, producing the latest innovations in information technology, semiconductors and clean technology. It is also a melting pot for immigrants who come to America seeking a new life for themselves and their children. Scores of engineers come to Silicon Valley to work, learn and connect with people from other countries. Japanese manufacturers work with Israeli software engineers and are financed and managed by American administrators in a fusion of talents and innovation that no other region or nation has ever produced.

I observed two principles at work in Silicon Valley – economic opportunity and reward for effort – and I think of these as the very principles that can, and are, revolutionizing our region, especially in Israel. They offer great potential for peace among peoples and provide the answer as to why a Zionist State is good for Israel's minorities, for a future Palestinian state, and for the other Arab countries in the region.

The story of my own Bedouin family illustrates this truth. It was through their alliance with the emerging Jewish State that the Bedouins began to transcend the isolation that was part of their nomadic history. My family, too, has reaped the benefits of this alliance, receiving health care, education, job training, and pensions. We minorities living in Israel can be our country's best ambassadors, helping to fulfill Herzl's vision – the world's recognition of the full legitimacy of the Jewish State. True justice and equity will be good for all Israelis. We must all do our part to make that happen.

What about the question of alleged Israeli apartheid? Even after two years in San Francisco, I still can't understand why Israel-bashers continue this assault. They say Israel is an apartheid state. My response is: Never. Jews and Arabs use the same buses, clinics, government offices, universities, theaters, restaurants, soccer fields, and beaches. All Israeli citizens, regardless of religion or ethnic origins, are equal before the law, the same law that accords full political, civil, and human rights to its entire population, including its more than one million Arab citizens, some of whom serve in the Israeli parliament. Israel is the only country in the world to have sought out and brought to its shores, entirely on its own initiative, tens of thousands of black Africans for purposes other than slavery, granting them full citizenship.

If the charges of racism are directed specifically against Israel's right of return, we better look at others for reflection and comparison. The Armenian constitution seeks "the protection of Armenian historical and cultural values located in other countries" and permits individuals of "Armenian origin" to acquire citizenship through "a simplified procedure." The Lithuanian constitution proclaims, "Everyone who is ethnically Lithuanian has the right to settle in Lithuania." Identical provisions exist in the Ukrainian and Polish constitutions.

If the ire of Israel's enemies is aroused by the fact that Israel is a Jewish State, why do they not direct their anger against Britain, a Christian state, with an official Anglican Church, Anglican monarch, and Protestant state education system? There are other Christian states with significant non-Christian minorities (specifically Muslims, many of whom seem unwelcome), such as Germany, the Netherlands, Denmark and Sweden. This, without mentioning the many countries whose names start with "Islamic Republic of …" or "Arab Republic of …" all of whom are vocal supporters of propaganda claiming Israel is an Apartheid state.

So, what do Americans really know about Israel? Or about their own country for that matter? At the end of

December 2008, Israel began an operation against Hamas in Gaza. The protests and negative comments that we at the consulate received were indescribable. They took place on all fronts – in the media, in street protests, in phone calls, and email messages. What was interesting is that most emails and phone calls to us began, "Hello, my name is … and I am Jewish." My immediate response would always be, "Thanks for calling and for your message. I'm Muslim, and I'm Israeli."

The mainstream press in the United States is often overly antagonistic toward Israel and this portrayal not only increases criticism but also misleads the American public, who, in fact, share so many values with Israelis. This misrepresentation is dangerous to both our peoples.

One might ask – as indeed many have – whether a person such as me, who is not Jewish, but a Muslim Arab, can represent the State of Israel today? The answer is yes. I know now, more than ever before, what the deleterious effects of mute indifference are, and I am therefore resolute. History will not tolerate our silence. Israel's right to exist is my right and my people's right, just as Israel's destiny is our shared destiny. But just as history demands that I fight for Israel, history also will not tolerate a generation of Jews who are complacent or do not care enough to get involved.

The operation against Hamas started two days after Christmas, the day that marks the birth of Jesus Christ, born in Nazareth, Israel. I wonder how many Americans contemplate the significance of Israel on that day? How many Americans know or have met an Israeli in their life? What do Americans know of Islam and the Muslim world? Too many Americans still believe that the mainstream Muslim majority shares the beliefs of its extremist minorities. Can we be confident that Americans know enough to maintain peace and the American reputation throughout the world?

Perhaps it is time to consider the flip side of the situation – to consider how America is seen through the eyes of Israeli Bedouins. To them, America represents hope for the world. People everywhere look to America as the best example of how mankind can live together in peace with the promise of liberty under the rule of law. Opportunity abounds. American power – military, economic, cultural – has become the central reality to which all others respond. The English (or really, the American) language has become the global tongue, particularly among young people who wish to work in the multi-national corporations that link the global economic system. Simply put, whether for good or for bad, America and its values and actions determine much of the reality for the rest of us. People live or die based on where and how leaders in the United States exert power.

Countries like South Korea, Taiwan, Iraq, Afghanistan and yes, Israel, benefit from U.S. alliances and military support. Other places in Africa, Asia and the Middle East suffer the consequences of war and strife without U.S. attention. No country in history has done more for other people than the United States. Not everyone who has benefited from American generosity and support has been thankful, but we in Israel have been thankful and we are America's strategic allies.

Israelis look to Americans as their only consistent friends, the ones who understand and support us, and, in the final analysis, will stand by us in times of need. For all our small disagreements, Israelis never doubt America's commitment and friendship.

Muslims in Western Societies

While lecturing in the Bay Area, I had the opportunity to meet with Muslim leaders. I assumed that if we in Israel found it hard to negotiate with Arab and Muslim leaders in the Middle East, where the conflict is political rather than religious, then perhaps here, in the West, it would be easier to speak with those influenced by Western values. And, I thought, who better than me to do it? So I initiated a dialogue with them. I must admit that many of the Arab and Muslim leaders were hesitant in the beginning and suspicious about an Israeli Bedouin Muslim diplomat. (Is such a thing even possible – all that in one package?) But they were very respectful, and with those whom I interacted, suspicion quickly turned into friendship. Even though we were not able to magically solve our differences, I learned a great deal about their status here in America. This what I observed in my dialogues with them.

My first impression was that many people ponder the question of Muslim extremism, but rarely do they talk openly with Muslims about it. Among themselves, and in the media, Christians and Jews express the concern that there is a rising tide of Muslim hatred on a collision course with Western values and democracy. For their part, Muslims wonder how much the average American really knows about Islam and the Muslim community. Many Americans clearly believe that the mainstream Muslim majority holds the same beliefs as the extremists.

Simply put, the question is: Are Muslims capable of being successfully absorbed into Western democracies as productive, loyal citizens? I cannot speak about Europe where this is a paramount question, but it is certain that many Americans are quick to make harsh generalizations about Arabs and Muslims, yet most can barely define the differences between them, or within them. Bedouin culture, for example, is conservative, insular and alien to western culture. We are tied to family, tribe, and village. Women are not sexually liberated, and men are responsible for providing support to their families. Along with strict sexual mores, there are also strong prohibitions against alcohol, gambling, drugs, and many other habits that are easily accepted and tolerated in Western societies. This is in part because, like many Muslim societies, the Bedouin developed in harsh desert climates, so "civilized" activities of art, music, literature, performance, and dance were not as refined or highly developed as in the West. We love our music, dance, stories, and art, but they are folk arts, not the high performance arts found in concert halls and museums. However, unlike many Muslim and Arab societies, Bedouins are not extroverted; we tend to be reticent to speak. We measure our worth not in GDP, achievement, and erudition, but rather by love, mutual support, and cohesiveness. This is a very powerful concept.

Picture a group of Bedouin workers who each takes his own food and places it on a mat in front of the group. One may have bread, another olives, a third cheese, a fourth some goat's milk, and so on. When each has contributed his individual items, there is a feast before them. All now eat together with no distinction as to who brought what, but rather as a family sharing what little they have with an open heart and friendship.

For Americans, learning about Middle Eastern cultures mushroomed only after the horrible events of 9/11. Following that event, language schools, research centers and university departments were started around the country for the teaching, research, and analysis of Islamic civilizations with the goal of understanding this religion, its history, and what lies behind it.

Muslims throughout America feel threatened, particularly Arab Muslims, simply because they are Muslims.

Obviously, there are Muslims who are terrorists, and the fact that terror in the name of the religion started in Muslim and Arab societies is a matter that warrants deep research. But Islam at its core is a religion of tolerance and respect. The Koran calls for respecting Jews and Christians and their religions. The misuse of its language by radical Muslims is wrong and does not faithfully represent Islam. It is the responsibility of all moderate Muslims to denounce any use of violence against innocent people as well as attempts to justify it in the name of Islam. There is often great misunderstanding about what is stated in the Koran regarding these issues. In most cases, their agenda is about land and power, not religious ideology. The unanswered question is why radical extremism, and support for terrorism, are able to take root and thrive in Muslim societies.

But back to Israel. What a Jew sees as the ingathering of the exiles and the miracle of modern Israel, the Israeli Arab may view as rule by a conquering nation. His values, based on honor and extended family or clan, may be hard for Westerners to comprehend, but these values are centered in Arab culture.

There are also the practical matters of day-to-day existence. In Israel, Arabs are simply trying to improve their lives and communities, and many – particularly the youth – are not stuck in a time warp as victims, even with their sense of historic misfortune. They must constantly navigate the different threads that constitute their lives, and that navigation is not without its contradictions.

So, is there Israeli Arab resentment? Sure, there is.
This question begs the larger question: Can Muslims
be good citizens in Western societies? Of course they can.
It is the predominant way of integrated life in Israel. There
is no reason to believe that this ability cannot be translated
to Western societies. When looking at examples in Israel,
go to Haifa, where Jews, Arabs, Baha'i, and all varieties of
people live in peace and harmony. Haifa, the pluralistic
city, is blessed with tolerance, diversity, and peace. Further north, in the western Galilee, see Nahariya Hospital,
which serves all of northwestern Israel. The Hospital CEO
is an Arab, and proud Israeli. Other Israeli Arab doctors,
nurses, and administrators work with their Israeli Jewish
counterparts to treat an equally diverse population. At
the Nahariya Hospital you see Israel – all of Israel – at its
best. There are many such examples in Israel. They are
models for the future of inter-ethnic relationships, not just
in Israel, but worldwide; they are the answer. May these
examples flourish and spread throughout Israel. I hope
that someday you will be able to visit Haifa or Nahariya
Hospital and remark on how unexceptional it is, compared
to the rest of Israel.

Building bridges is never easy, particularly when there
is so much misunderstanding between peoples. But my
experience in America, my experience as a Bedouin in
Israel, my whole life, in fact, drives me to continue the
work of connecting people and building those bridges of
understanding in the Middle East.

Chapter 6
After All, Remaining Bedouin …

Today, as I peer into the mirror, I see a mature and complex man returning my gaze, a man who has had many unusual, special, formative experiences. International travel in recent years has enabled me to see other cultures, peoples, and traditions. In most of my travels I have been searching for myself, and I still am, in a way. My journey may never end, yet its conclusion already seems clear: I will forever be a Bedouin, the shepherd boy running up the hills of Khawalid, making friends and building the future with my fellow Israeli Jewish kibbutzniks, but also with a moral responsibility to raise a young generation of Bedouins who will adhere to their values, heritage, and tradition. Above all, as I've come to understand all that has shaped me, I have finally come to accept all that I am.

As my journey continues, however, I feel I am still paying a personal price and sacrifice. It was over ten years ago that my father began chiding me, "We're getting older, Ish, and we're not seeing enough of you here. Do what you want to do, but get married!" My career choice, my travel, my removal from the village life – all this stands between me and a traditional home with a wife and kids. Even so, I know it will happen. My saga with S hasn't ended yet, despite the years that have passed by, but even as I write this, she finally seems to be coming to terms with the idea of leaving the village of her birth. It's just a matter of time before she jumps into the cold water and begins to swim. When this happens, and only in this way, will I know that my personal mission has been accomplished!

But the truth is, no matter how aware one is of what one wants and where one would like to be, we really don't have control of the events that shape our lives. Life sometimes propels us in directions we never conceived, to places and horizons for which we're not prepared. As for me, I will continue as I always have, always the Bedouin, attached to tradition and yet apart from it, who, as my young kibbutznik friends like to say, will always keep "looking for myself."

I could have grown up to be a shepherd like my father, which would have been easier, for sure, but I'm proud of what I've chosen to do. My country depends on me to do my duty, and I will not disappoint. My future will surely include two important goals. First, I will help seek the peace and security necessary to build a modern Israel, with a prosperous future full of hope for better days. Second, I will put great effort into raising a young generation of Bedouins who honor their values and heritage and traditions.

I believe those two goals reflect something important about who I am, who I have become – a man who straddles the modern and traditional and who has learned the value of both. There is a certain wonderful absurdity in the idea that I came all the way to America, land of the free, to realize that my identity will always lie in the eye of the storm, in the space between old and new that is itself a sort of miracle.

I have changed so much since my first day in America. I love to imagine the boy that I was, so unfamiliar with urban living, jumping down on the subway tracks, sidestepping the deadly third rail, climbing up the other side of the platform like a Bedouin Crocodile Dundee! In a strange city, unfamiliar with the customs and language, I felt invisible to everyone around me. Lost. But even then, deep inside, I felt strong and proud of who I was and where I came from.

Perhaps the most important part of my evolution has been this acceptance of who I am. I am a Muslim-Bedouin-Israeli. I know that I will always live in the heart of controversy. I will be a stranger in every community – Jew, Muslim, Arab world, American. Even those who see me positively may be suspicious that I do not share their values. I will always wrestle with alienation and loneliness. But I'm okay with that because I know who I am. I believe in who I am. And so, from here, where? What's next? What should be done?

With the understanding that it is only through economic opportunity and reward for effort that hope can flourish, and that people can engage their energies in positive endeavors that benefit themselves and their societies, I have hope for the future. Most importantly, we all must work to achieve peace in Israel and equality among its citizens. We who reside in free societies have to work to assure our children live in harmony, to turn back the tide of hate, intolerance, and ignorance that inflame all sides of the conflicts of our time.

As I consider all there is to do in my own country and on the world stage, I am struck not only by the enormity of the task at hand, but also by the possibilities ahead. The road is daunting, but I do not feel discouraged. Against all odds, I find myself asking: When will Israel have its own Barack Obama? I believe all minorities have that same aspiration to lead, as we're all Israelis, too. And I believe it is possible. I live as a minority in my own country and have certainly suffered for my mixed identity, but I am actually grateful for this, because it allowed me sight beyond my own culture, beyond the things that divide us, to a new awareness of the real human dimensions that bind us, and this in turn has enabled me to make connections to people across cultures, people I would never have otherwise known. This is the source of my hope, this is the path to my future.

And so, I end my reflections with two stories that capture the spirit I have tried to convey: one Arab and one Jewish.

An Arab Story:

An old man is dying and asks his son to fulfill his last request. He wants him to go to every village and build a home. The son takes all the money his father has left him and commences building a house in every village he can find, but then the money runs out. Discouraged that he cannot fulfill his father's request, he sits forlorn on a bench. An old man sees him and asks him why he is so sad. The son tells the old man the story – how his father asked him to build a home in every village and how there is no more money left with which to do it – and is surprised when the old man starts to laugh. "Why are you laughing at me?" asks the son. The old man replies, "I am not mocking you, my son, but you did not understand your father's request. When he said to build a home in each village he did not mean to build a house. What he wanted is for you to make a friend in each place you go, so that you are at home in every place you travel."

A Jewish Story:

In the ancient land of Israel, the Temple in Jerusalem was destroyed on two separate occasions: the Babylonians destroyed the first; the Romans destroyed the second. The ancient Israelites believed that their God dwelt in the Temple. For two thousand years, those living in exile far from their beloved land of Israel yearned to return to Jerusalem and build a third Temple. However, over the centuries the yearning for the Temple changed from the building a particular structure in a particular place to a metaphorical Temple where God dwells. That Temple in Spirit would be where the Jews and humanity would become holy and blessed, ushering in the messianic era. This story is told to foretell the spirit of that era:

A long time ago in Jerusalem, there lived two brothers who were both farmers. They tended their crops on opposite sides of a hilltop. One brother was married and had a large family. The other lived alone. They farmed the land and harvested equal amounts of produce. Every night the two brothers, each in his own home at opposite ends of the field, would lie awake in thought. The brother with the large family would think to himself, "My brother is alone, and has no one to take care of him. Surely he needs more of the crop than I." Meanwhile, the single brother wondered, "My brother has many children to feed. Surely he and his wife need more of the crop than I." And so each night, long after midnight, the married man would gather bundles of wheat, carry them across the field and quietly place them among his brother's supply. And likewise, the single man would gather some of his bundles late at night and secretly deliver them to his married brother. Years passed, each brother unaware of the other's generosity.

One clear, starry night, the two brothers met as they carried their bundles of wheat across the field. Realizing what the other had been doing all these years, they dropped their produce, held out their arms, and embraced. Weeping together, they realized the true meaning of brotherly love.

One can choose to understand these stories as the possibility that Jews and Arabs will one day make each other feel at home in Israel. In the words of Martin Luther King, I, too, have a dream, that in the future, children on both sides will start playing together and going to school together. Both will be responsible to make Israel as a better place. Both will turn the differences between them into bridges of understanding and channels of coexistence. No one is saying that this will be easy. People on both sides will have to work hard, be patient and resolute, but I truly believe it is "Mission Possible." Palestinians will have their own independent state, led by a democratic regime, and develop an open, liberal society. Israeli Arabs living in Israel, including all the non-Jewish minorities – Bedouins, Druze – will live in Israel as equals, creating a brotherhood in which we all take care of each other. And together we will also build a bridge of understanding between us, Israel, and our neighbors the Arab countries.

Photo © David Blumenfeld
www.blumenfeld.com

Paul Curran – creator of the portrait image